BREAKING CORPORATE SILENCE
HOW HIGH-INFLUENCE LEADERS CREATE CULTURES OF VOICE

DEDICATION

In memory of my father, Zaven Bogosian, a consummate leader, great violinist and life-long learner who garnered the emotional commitment of all his employees. He always assumed positive intent.

RB

With thankfulness to those leaders who, with respectful intention, enable their employees to work with full and fulfilling engagement. To my husband Mike, who lives the definition of partner and models authenticity and integrity. And to Rob, whom I consistently continue to admire for his depth of character and commitment.

CMC

BREAKING CORPORATE SILENCE
HOW HIGH-INFLUENCE LEADERS CREATE CULTURES OF VOICE

DR. ROB BOGOSIAN
CHRISTINE MOCKLER CASPER, MBA

BREAKING CORPORATE SILENCE

Printed in the United States of America.

BCS Publishing
Dennis, Massachusetts
First Edition
ISBN 978-0-9914876-3-9 (Hardcover)
ISBN 978-0-9914876-1-5 (Paperback)

TABLE OF CONTENTS

CONCLUSION:

LIST OF DIAGRAMS, EXHIBITS, AND TABLES

CHAPTER FIVE

CONCLUSION

NOTE TO OUR READERS

The authors make no representations or warranties whatsoever as to the accuracy, completeness, or suitability for any purpose of the information contained in this book. Although every effort has been made to ensure that the information in this book was correct at the time of publication, the authors do not assume and hereby disclaim any liability to any party for any loss, damage, or disruption caused by errors or omissions in the book, whether such errors or omissions result from negligence, accident, or any other cause. Further, the authors hereby disclaim any liability to any party for any loss or damage resulting from the use, application, or interpretation of the material in the book. Names and identifying details have been changed to protect the privacy of individuals and organizations.

The information contained within this book is intended to educate and inform business leaders. If you wish to apply the principles contained in this book, you assume full responsibility for your actions and we urge you to consult with the appropriate professionals within your organization prior to implementing any changes.

INTRODUCTION

The timing of this book could not be more critical. There is no other book that we know of, written in layman's language, that addresses the omnipresent crisis that is **corporate silence**. And make no mistake: it is a crisis. As organizations strive to deal with turbulence, disruptive technological advances, and knowledge acquisition and transfer, now more than ever, leaders need guidance on how to face reality and demonstrate leadership practices that capture and cultivate their greatest resource – the emotional commitment of their workforce. In order to enhance innovation, develop personal power, and engage employees in ways that protect your business and organizational goals, you need to break corporate silence wherever you find it.

Breaking Corporate Silence is based on rigorous research by Dr. Rob Bogosian on the phenomenon of employee silence, and the extensive global and executive development experience of Christine Mockler Casper and Dr. Rob Bogosian. Each chapter will help to improve your ability to demonstrate what we call High-Influence Leadership® practices that can move your organization from a culture of silence to a culture of voice.

High-Influence Leaders encourage and sustain cultures of voice. When your organization has a culture of voice, the workforce won't hold back important work-related information that could inform key decisions and problem resolutions. A culture of voice can prevent operational surprises that lead to chaos and counterproductive work behaviors amounting to waste.

A culture of voice occurs when each employee experiences the safety, confidence, and trust they need to contribute their fullest, resulting in open, honest, and healthy communication, innovative problem solving, knowledge transfer, and real potential for sustainable competitive advantage. A culture of silence, by contrast, is one where employees, regardless of their hierarchical position, willfully withhold important work-related information. They may perform their jobs, but they will do so as a matter of obedience or resignation. They may analyze your words and actions with suspicion; they may not grant you or anyone else the benefit of the doubt. The most common causes of employee silence are specific leadership behaviors that result in employees withholding information, either for fear of retribution or simply because they have no faith that their contribution will be accepted and respected. They won't share their expertise; they won't fully absorb or apply knowledge that comes their way. Their success will be self-serving, nothing more. Your success will not matter to them (and in fact, they may harbor a desire to see you fail). The company's success or failure may not even appear on their radar.

Breaking Corporate Silence explores the dynamics and causes of a corporate culture of voice and a culture of silence[1] and how your leadership behaviors elicit and sustain one or the other. Over time, a culture of voice expands employee discretionary effort required to achieve an organization's goals. Esprit de corps flourishes. Our vision is for every company to have a culture of voice where associates willfully participate in the process of personal and organizational achievement. We hope to add the term culture of voice to the leadership vernacular and for every company to work toward minimizing or eliminating cultures of silence.

No matter where you are on the corporate ladder —Manager, Vice President, Senior Vice President, Executive Vice President— you can't do your job as effectively as possible unless you have the support of those above AND below you. You know that, at least in theory. But what does "support" really mean on a day-to-day basis, and how can you obtain and sustain it from your associates? Support (from associates) means the amount of effort the people around you are willing to expend to meet organizations' goals and advance business objectives *beyond fulfilling the basic requirements of their jobs*. You may be in charge of a particular initiative, team, or function, but your employee culture[2] and how you influence it will determine the extent to which you succeed.

---

1   Morrison & Milliken, 2000

2   Slap, S., 2010

Their discretionary effort[3] is elastic, and it can stretch in your favor or not. If you can say with great confidence that in good times and bad the people around you will put forth that extra effort, then skim through the rest of this book. If you're not sure—in fact, if you suspect in any way that your employees, associates, and higher-ups have an "every-man-for-himself" mindset—then you should read on more closely because this book explores how cultures of silence are created, how (employee) discretionary effort expands and contracts, and your role in this elasticity.

YOUR ROLE

Your behavior, on a daily basis, supports either a culture of voice or a culture of silence[4]. (Maybe you do both!) This book assesses the extent to which you are creating one, or the other, and offers an array of tools to help you develop and sustain a climate of voice.

Breaking Corporate Silence deals with the state (not trait) of leadership that encourages voice or elicits silence. It will *not* try to make extraverts out of introverts, or vice versa. Voice and silence in this context have nothing to do with whether you are by nature a quiet person or someone who is bubbly, chatty, or charismatic. Quiet leaders can elicit great discretionary effort and encourage knowledge transfer among their colleagues, superiors, and direct reports. People who are more naturally talkative can elicit climates of silence. There's no link between your preference for extraversion or introversion and a culture of voice or silence. What matters, instead, is the extent to which your influence helps others feel significant, safe, respected, and valued. This book will help you understand how others in your organization experience and perceive your actions, and it will help you improve your leadership practices and others' perceptions. It will strengthen your ability to self-reflect and gain deep insights into the ways your management practices impact others and as a result, influence business results.

---

3 Yankelovich & Immerwahr, 1984.

4 Morrison & Milliken, 2000

We have synthesized a set of six High-Influence Leadership® practices that encourage voice and accelerate knowledge transfer in companies. *High (positive) Influence Leaders* are fully aware of their actions in the moment and after the moment. They can quickly self-correct when their influence is faltering and do so in a way that strengthens associate commitment. It is our belief that every leader, with proper guidance and development, can become a High-Influence Leader that results in a culture of voice.

A CHAPTER MAP

The book has four formal parts.

Part I: The Culture (chapters one and two) explains in depth the concept of a culture of silence versus a culture of voice (chapter one) and then offers you assessments to help you assess your organizational culture (chapter two).

Part II: The Leader (chapters three and four) takes the same approach—first with theory, as chapter three examines the six High-Influence Leadership® practices, then with practice, as chapter four explores High-Influence Leadership® behaviors that foster cultures of voice.

Part III: The Insight & Impact (chapter five) focuses on how leaders can sustain a culture of voice. Chapter five explores how leaders can keep their fingers on the pulse of their leadership practices and the resulting influence on the organization's culture.

Conclusion: A challenge to you, our readers. We believe strongly that if you commit to fostering a culture of voice in your organization, you will be able to do it. We hope (and also believe) that the ideas and methods offered in this book will help you make it happen.

WHY WE WROTE THIS BOOK

We both have a passion for learning with a purpose, and our purpose, for as long as either of us can remember in our professional lives, has been to identify and develop resources—particularly centered around motivational and communication tools and techniques—to help people and organizations become the best they can be. We are driven to help managers become High-Influence Leaders and to fully comprehend the impact of their behavior on the employee culture, their peers, and their businesses.

But the path that led us to write this book wasn't linear. We had already been friends and colleagues for more than 20 years, in fact, when we decided to collaborate on this project. We were first introduced at State Street Corporation in Boston. Rob was a program manager responsible for development of State Street's middle- to senior-level leaders. Christine was a trusted consultant who helped State Street's leaders develop their professional skills. From the start, we shared our views and opinions about organizational health, organizational culture dynamics, leadership development, and the challenges and successes of the thousands of managers with whom we worked. Rob's career progression then extended to two other global, publically held corporations before he launched his own consulting practice, RVB Associates, in 2005. Meanwhile, Christine expanded her corporate business, Communication, Motivation & Management, Inc., with a focus on Emotional Intelligence (EI).

We stayed in touch and continued to collaborate. And in the years that followed, we had the privilege of working together in some of the largest and most well-respected organizations in the world, including State Street Corporation, Compaq/Digital, Santander Bank, Citizens Financial Group, and Wells Fargo (Wachovia).

Over time, we became increasingly interested in the idea of companies having what we called "cultures of silence." Then, in 2008, Rob began his doctoral work at The George Washington University, Washington, DC, focusing on this phenomenon, its causes, and consequences.

We were dismayed, but not surprised, by how Rob's research results confirmed our theories, and we started mapping those results against what we'd seen in the leadership development arena. We started talking about clients whose organizations suffered because of lack of discretionary effort and slow knowledge transfer which we found was a key symptom of a culture of silence. We realized that with Rob's rigorous research and Christine's MBA and client experiences, we were at a point where we knew we could offer our insights in the form of a book. We both felt—and still feel—that with our awareness of "silence," we have a responsibility to share what we've learned.

This book is intended for the leader practitioner. It is meant to serve as a body of knowledge and research from Rob's research study on (the lived experience) organizational silence and from our collective experiences developing, coaching, and consulting with thousands of managers around the globe.

CHAPTER ONE
CULTURES OF SILENCE, CULTURES OF VOICE, AND THE HIGH-INFLUENCE LEADER

When your employees are silent—when you aren't hearing any ideas or complaints—it might mean that they're busy and happy. But it might also mean that some critical communication channels—the ones that move information that would improve processes and foster innovation—are blocked. It may mean that your organization suffers from having a culture of silence, which can lead to breakdowns in customer relationships, a loss of talented employees, and even disastrous product or service failures. It is every leader's obligation to understand the phenomenon of silence in the workplace, the causes, and consequences.

We begin with a set of cases that describe the lived experiences of silence in various organizations and industries. Our research shows that cultures of silence are not found in any one organization type or industry. Rather, the silence phenomenon is prevalent across organizations, industries, and national cultures, and is mostly created by leader-employee interactions. As you read each case, you will gain a sense of the leader-employee interactions that resulted in a culture of silence. Then, you can begin to reflect on your own leader practices to assess the extent to which they may be eliciting silence or encouraging voice.

The cases:

On April 15, 1912, the glorious S.S. Titanic struck an iceberg and sank on its maiden voyage, killing 1517 of the 2223 people who had been on board. Incredibly, the Titanic had just 20 lifeboats, enough to accommodate only 42 percent of the passengers and crew. Perhaps more incredibly, that was legal; the number of lifeboats that a ship was required to have (and their capacities) was based on the gross register tonnage of a ship rather than on the number of people who would be aboard.

In the Senate testimony given after the disaster, Joseph Bruce Ismay, Chairman of the White Star Line and Titanic's owner, admitted that the company's senior leaders hadn't paid much attention to the issue. He stated that in production meetings, "We discussed the colors of the first class carpet for three hours and the lifeboat capacity issue for 15 minutes" (Titanic Disaster, United States Inquiry Report).

This despite the fact that some engineers had long suspected the ship could sink under certain circumstances. Why hadn't they sounded a forceful warning? Examination of the Senate testimonials reveals that engineers were put off by White Star Line leaders' attitudes. Given the time that Ismay and his team had spent discussing Titanic's appearance and comfort compared to the time they spent examining the ship's safety risks, perhaps the engineers felt their warnings would be futile. It seems certain the approach that leadership took contributed to the engineers' reticence.

***

On April 20, 2010, a British Petroleum oil well in the Gulf of Mexico exploded, killing 11 workers and spilling millions of gallons of crude oil into the Gulf of Mexico. British Petroleum had permission from the federal Minerals Management Service to drill for oil "without first getting required permits from the National Oceanic and Atmospheric Administration that assesses threats to endangered species — and despite strong warnings from scientists at that agency about the impact the drilling was likely to have on the gulf."[1] According to the National Wildlife Federation, "More than 8,000 birds, sea turtles, and marine mammals were found injured or dead in the six months after the spill. The long-term damage caused by the oil and the nearly two million gallons of chemical dispersants used on the spill may not be known for years."[2]

Scientists at the National Oceanic and Atmospheric Administration, along with a cadre of concerned environmentalists, frequently warned of

1   U.S. Said to Allow Drilling Without Needed Permits By IAN URBINA
2   Retrieved July 15, 2014, from https://www.nwf.org/What-We-Do/Protect-Habitat/Gulf-Restoration/Oil-Spill/Effects-on-Wildlife.aspx

the dangers of drilling in the region. Their actions were futile. Senior-level managers from the Minerals Management Service gave BP permission to drill anyway, an action that ultimately resulted in a disaster that is said to have reached epic proportions.

***

Spring 2014: In a GM-funded report by former U.S. Attorney Anton Valukas, Chief Executive Officer Mary Barra acknowledges that the auto-maker's decade-plus failure to recall cars that had defective ignition switches (resulting in at least a dozen deaths) reflects "a pattern of incompetence and neglect." According to the Wall Street Journal,[3] Valukas reported a "troubling disavowal of responsibility" at GM, and Barra was cited for describing a behavior called the "GM Nod," or a practice whereby employees seem to agree on a course of action but then fail to act.

Other published articles from the same period in 2014 revealed a list of words that GM senior executives had instructed employees to avoid via a 2008 presentation designed to train employees how to communicate with one another about potential safety issues. These words included: "Titanic," "powder keg," "failure," and "serious." Employees were also provided with guidance about appropriate substitutions. Instead of "defect," for example, they were told to say that something "does not perform to design." Instead of "problem," they were told to sub in a word like "issue" or "matter."

An article by Peter Valdes-Dapena, published by CNN Money on May 17, 2014, reported that "National Highway Traffic Safety Administration Acting Administrator David Friedman criticized GM for the presentation during a press conference Friday [May 16th]. Friedman said that, in telling employees to avoid certain language when writing about safety issues, GM was discouraging open and free discussion of potential problems."

The Titanic, the BP oil spill, and the 2014 revelations about GM's ignition switch fiasco are extreme examples. But a culture of silence does at least some damage in any organization where it thrives. It causes managers to ignore valuable input from third parties. It causes them to

---

3   Bennett, J. & Lublin, J. S. (2014). GM Recall Probe to Blame Cultural Failings. Wall Street Journal.

marginalize internal knowledge. It compels employees to stop short of expending any discretionary effort. Reduced to its essentials, it prevents the flow of potentially critical information in all sorts of organizations on a daily basis, increasing the risk of poor decision making and any negative results that could ensue.

What are the root causes of a culture of silence? Is your organization vulnerable? And are you, as a manager, inadvertently fostering these "silent" behaviors that could one day cause a very loud negative event?

By contrast, what conditions foster cultures of voice in which employees speak freely and offer a bounty of discretionary effort, going out of their way to ensure that important information gets where it needs to go, and where the company—*their* company—is stronger because of their efforts? How can you ensure that your organization encourages a culture of voice?

This book seeks to answer all of those questions. In the coming chapters, we'll uncover the causes of cultures of silence and their antidotes. We'll help you figure out whether your organization has such a culture. We'll show you the kinds of leadership practices that encourage cultures of voice and help you determine which of those practices will work best for you and for your company. We'll also share a number of ideas and exercises to help you build a strong culture of voice and sustain it over the long term.

THREE PRIMARY CAUSES OF EMPLOYEE SILENCE

Our research shows that a culture of silence and its flip side—the infinitely more desirable culture of voice— share three primary causes:

1. Leaders' and managers' underlying **beliefs** about their roles and responsibilities, about how they ought to present themselves, and about employee mindsets and tendencies. ("A leader should know what is best for the company." "Organizational conformity is a sign of strength." "Conflict and disagreement are a sign of weakness or lack of commitment on the leader's part." "A leader's job is to facilitate others' work." "Disagreement is a sign of creativity and strength." "Leaders have to protect their people.")

2. The **values** that those beliefs compel (integrity, achievement, timeliness, order, collaboration, transparency).

3. The **behaviors** that manifest themselves in a manager's style, stemming largely from his or her beliefs and values. (For example, controlling the decisions and problem-solving processes or communicating on a (perceived) "need-to-know" basis.)

In practice, these three "causes" are actually both causes and results. They feed on one another, and as one grows in strength, they spread through an organization until they create either a culture of silence or a culture of voice. Importantly, though, there are few absolute "right" or "wrong" beliefs, values, and behaviors that cause either a culture of silence or a culture of voice.

Leadership styles tend to be dichotomous and fall into two categories, those that focus on the work and those that focus on the people. Work-focused leadership styles tend to be autocratic, task-oriented, and use a centralized decision making method. People-oriented leaders are more considerate of their associates, share in decision making, and provide support to associates (Bass, 1985).

These dichotomous styles can affect a leader's behaviors in different ways. The people-oriented, or "democratic-style," leader seeks input, offers relevant information, makes the ultimate decisions to facilitate progress, and offers encouragement and praise to associates. The authoritarian-style leader is inclined to determine and announce all policies affecting group members and tends to dictate processes.

One would think that we're leading up to say that the people-oriented style is preferable and leads to a culture of voice and that the work-focused style leads inevitably to a culture of silence. But that's not the case! Neither style is all good or all bad.

It's clear that a leader must choose or adapt elements of one or another management style according to a number of variables, such as task complexity, the requirements of the business, the risk associated with any given tasks or projects, and the employee's ability and experience. The key is to figure out which style is your "default" style and what the implications are of that style on the people you're leading. How does it all add up?

BELIEFS, VALUES, AND BEHAVIORS FROM THE LEADER'S POINT OF VIEW

Beliefs, values, and behaviors—what might these look like in practice, from the leader's point of view? Consider this hypothetical scenario:

> The new department head believes fervently that it is her job to provide seamless solutions for the rest of the organization. To do so, she assumes it is her job to

determine what those solutions ought to be and then direct her employees to complete tasks to develop and maintain them. That's what they're paying her the big bucks for—to be the leader.

Beliefs

She believes that *"if you give them an inch, they'll take a mile,"* and so she has made it clear that she wants to see people working at their desks by 8:30 a.m. each day and that she doesn't want them to decorate their offices and cubicles with a lot of clutter about their home lives. She prefers that her staff maintain a professional attitude at all times and keep their personal lives to themselves.

Values

Valuing structure and control, she thinks that running her department properly means all of her employees show that they are "team players" and that they are "on task" at all times. She sets deadlines accordingly and holds staff meetings at which she checks the "punch list" and assigns next-stage projects. She is mindful of distractions and worries a lot when conversations at meetings get off point. She is fond of saying, "Let's take that offline," meaning that whatever that ancillary topic is, she doesn't want it to slow down the meeting and prefers to discuss it privately or with a smaller group at another time.

Behaviors

She has told her staff that her door "is always open," and she means it. But in order to see her, staff members must generally schedule an appointment with her assistant. Also, she spends most lunch times meeting with other executives in the managers' lunchroom, feeling that it is important for these individuals to get to know her and see her as a responsive colleague. She parks in a special section of the company lot reserved for managers. She assumes that her staff is happy; not many of them schedule appointments to voice concerns. Things seem to hum along as they should.

This executive thinks she is acting in the best interests of the company. But it's likely that she is inadvertently fostering a culture of silence. Her employees may be keeping their mouths shut about their ideas, or concerns, for fear of seeming as if they're not team players. They may be quiet because they perceive her autocratic approach as abusive. They may sense that she has drawn a line in the sand that she doesn't want them to cross. They may not want to "stand out," believing, because of this manager's behavior, that their best bet for survival in the company is to conform to the group and not make waves.

Now consider an alternate scenario:

Beliefs

The new head of the department believes fervently that it is her job to lead her staff by facilitating the process of developing an optimal solution. She schedules meetings to brainstorm ideas, makes the ultimate decision about which course of action to pursue, and then works with her staff to develop a reasonable timetable for executing their plan. She holds them to these timetables; the ability to set and stick to a timetable is reflected in performance reviews.

Values

Valuing teamwork, she eats lunch with other executives; valuing inclusion, she knows that it is important to know her colleagues and the people on the "next level and beyond" in the organization. But on Tuesdays, Wednesdays, and Fridays, she eats lunch in the department's conference room with anyone on her staff who wants to join.

Behaviors

She has appointed a project manager to oversee progress and ensure that the work being done on new initiatives doesn't compromise the department's daily operations. She checks in with this project manager regularly and helps that person adjust timetables as needed based on any new information that has come to her attention.

She parks in the same spot she's always parked in—long habit has her parking at the far end of the lot—and she usually spends the first 20 minutes of her day walking around the department, checking in, informally and randomly, with her staff.

It's far more likely that the conditions present in that second scenario foster a culture of voice. The staff members in this department have a higher probability of feeling valued and significant and have confidence that their boss relies on their contribution to the organization at large. This boss is also task-oriented and attentive to detail and deadline, but her behaviors are more balanced than those of the executive in the first example.

That's not to say that manager's lunchrooms and reserved parking spaces are necessarily evil harbingers or symptoms of a culture of silence. They're not. But all organizational symbolism (such as reserved parking, offices or open floor plan, executive lounges, and so forth) is related to leaders' perceptions and aspirations for their organization's culture and is clearly keyed into senior leaders' beliefs and resulting expectations of themselves and their staff members.

BELIEFS, VALUES, AND BEHAVIORS FROM THE EMPLOYEE'S POINT OF VIEW

Now consider a set of case examples that describe in detail how employees experience the phenomenon of silence. We've used pseudonyms to protect the anonymity of the managers profiled below, and we have edited some of the quotes for purposes of brevity and clarity. But the details are real. Bear in mind that these employees you're about to hear from have had different motivations for their silence. Some may feel a need to protect themselves. Some may be responding to a particular "trigger event," and some may be reacting to perceived group dynamics. Some have chosen silence as a means of retaliation against an action they felt was unjust.

Also bear in mind that *none of these employees have insight into the beliefs or values that are driving their bosses' behaviors.* They may have made assumptions based on incomplete and inaccurate views of their bosses' values and beliefs. Their own motivations (fear, a sense of futility) may be clouding their ability to think objectively.

Lee

Lee was an executive in a global financial services organization. She has an MBA and is an award-winning sportsperson.

"The new boss came on board, and I didn't speak up when this person was basically requiring us to hire certain people and fire others. The people that this person wanted us to fire hadn't done anything wrong— they were never on probation. It was like this person came in and wanted to bring in his/her own people. I kept silent because it was clear who was in charge, and this person had been verbally abusive. No one else seemed concerned that this person was torpedoing people and forcing them to leave."

"I remember this person made me fire some employees. I was in his office, and I was very upset (about this), crying. This person said, 'Don't take it personally, or you will kill yourself; this is what corporations do,' or something like that. I remember walking out of this person's office thinking, 'This is NOT what corporations do, and if you had to do this, there had to be a better way.' I hated it [firing someone], and I lost sleep for weeks. It was absolutely horrible because you know you have someone's livelihood in your hands."

"I began to feel like I could fight back and persevere, but then I realized that life is too short, and I couldn't stand to come to work any longer."

Lee left her job shortly thereafter and took a position with another firm.

> Lee's silence was defensive. Associates affected by trigger events often cannot accept or adjust to the powerlessness and threatening environment created by a new manager's power exhibition. Those who cannot make sense of the conditions that elicited their silence ultimately leave their companies because they see no other choice. The Society for Human Resource Management estimates that it costs companies approximately 22 percent of annual salary to replace a minimum-wage employee. The replacement cost percentage rises for positions higher in the hierarchical structure.

Isaac

Isaac is a bright, upwardly mobile senior-level leader with a promising future. As a manager in a financial organization on the brink of a strong growth trajectory, Isaac's role was a critical link to capital markets. Isaac had military experience and graduated from a top-ranked college in the United States. The military's strong ethics and values were a large part of Isaac's character: "In the military, you are taught that all you have is your integrity and honesty and to follow orders." Isaac's military training influenced his relationship with the boss: "I put a lot of trust in my boss — they know best, and I should try to be supportive. I worked with the boss, and I knew his style. I was accustomed to him, so I was used to this kind of stress."

Isaac was asked to make a presentation to a capital markets group that would essentially secure the funding that the company needed to grow. There was a lot resting on this presentation for Isaac, and he felt some pressure to perform. Isaac was asked to present an inflated analysis and an embellished financial conclusion that would satisfy the capital markets group and secure the required capital for growth: "The day before this meeting, a Director gave me a projection number to present which was grossly overstated. I didn't know where that number came from, but I didn't think it was truthful." Isaac was told to present the incorrect numbers to the meeting participants, and as a result, he was caught between a proverbial rock and hard place: "I felt trapped like I didn't have a choice." So, he remained silent about the truth for fear of losing his job.

Isaac assessed the risk of voicing the truth about financial projections to the meeting participants and remaining silent: "If I called them on it, it would be over because I would have been let go." Isaac felt pressured to collude with his superiors because if he disclosed the truth in the group setting, the firm's capital access would have been jeopardized: "I felt trapped to this [false] number but assumed that they wouldn't hold me to it." Isaac felt there was a lot riding on his silence and feared that without the capital injection, peers and subordinates could lose their jobs: "I felt responsible for whether or not the company would get the access to capital, the responsibility for the company, and to the people who could lose their jobs. I had to figure this out." Isaac made every effort to find a way to substantiate the "inflated" number.

Upon reflection, Isaac described this trigger event that elicited his silence as a turning point for him and a "good life lesson" linked to his core human values: "It was a good life lesson for me – to stand your ground." But he didn't. "I'm smarter now, and I would have told the truth or not attended any meeting where I had to stretch the truth." Isaac also altered his views about following orders and trusting authority: "After this experience, my whole approach is very different — you have to earn my loyalty. I don't give it freely anymore."

Isaac's silence was a result of decreased psychological safety. Associate effort contracts as a result of trigger events that elicit silence. Associates often feel threatened and conflicted about their personal values and contrary views. They responded to the threat by doing only what was essential in their current job.

Much has been researched and written about on the subject of leadership and the characteristics that make good leaders. However, there is not as much research on bad leadership. In all the study cases, silence was elicited by the actions of a leader mostly in a negative context and mostly when unhealthy power was asserted over the manager's subordinate.

The underlying message in most cases was one of power over subordinates with a common message experienced as, "Do as you are told." As a result, individuals describe feelings of betrayal, broken trust, experiencing maniacal behavior, shock, and disbelief.

Alex

Alex is an information technology manager in a higher education institution, a leader between 35-45 years of age. In her words:

"I had always given ideas. I was always vocal and making suggestions. My colleagues began to rely on my contributions. I brought a work issue to my boss on the side because she asked me not to discuss things in front of the group. So, I explained the issue and how I would go about solving it. She said, 'Okay, will you write it up for me? It's a really good idea.' So, I write it up, and in the next big staff meeting, she announces that she has an idea to solve the XYZ problem, and guess whose idea she presents? Mine! Next, she took the idea to her boss and several levels above, and this great idea now becomes her idea. My boss never gave me credit. I've been told in the past not to refute in public anything my boss says. So, in that instant, I decided to remain silent always."

"In fact, I disengaged completely. I'll do what I am told to do. I will do it to the best of my ability and not violate my personal

standards of work, but in terms of loyalty to the organization, commitment to the organization, to the manager, nothing."

"I thought this person demonstrated a lack of integrity and also just being lazy. This boss was using position and authority to say, 'You can't speak up about this.' My idea was stolen from me, and it damages the relationship because at this point, there is no trust, and we can't have a relationship."

Alex's silence was offensive. It was the result of her perception of the leader's action. The autocratic leader can shut down idea generation and as a result, have trouble gaining acceptance from others. When employees' attempts to voice concerns about significant work-related issues have negative reactions from superiors, they usually conclude that it is too risky to communicate bad information upward in the organization. This conclusion is socialized among the employee community and can result in a culture of silence.

Monica

Monica is a human resources expert in the field of development. She is an MBA and has worked in large global organizations for most of her career.

"Organizational offsite meetings are usually a time when teams assemble out of the day-to-day work setting to focus on a particular issue. Offsite sessions usually combine business and social dynamics and create a comfortable atmosphere where participants can speak their minds. But when I spoke up, asking for clarification on the rationale behind a decision that had been made by the senior team, my boss took me aside later and reprimanded me for speaking up."

"My boss told me I should have just done what I was told to do. The thing is, I'm not the type of a person to just do something without asking why."

"It was like I had broken some kind of code. I asked him if we could discuss the situation and if I could try to remedy it, but he wouldn't engage in the conversation. I felt as if I was no longer trusted. He communicated with me less; there was no more information or idea seeking with me. He just began to go around me, avoid me, and I felt betrayed, like I was on a black list."

"I felt a sense of loss. I used to be involved, and after this, our relationship went downhill, like I wasn't trusted anymore. It was like grieving the loss of someone; I was so sad. I began to doubt my capability and the choice to speak up. I wondered if I was really not good enough that someone (manager) has to tell me what to do all the time? I became much more guarded after that incident, and I am not a guarded person."

Monica's silence was the result of defensiveness. Aggressive and/or autocratic leadership behaviors affect employee's global feelings of self-worth (Crocker & Major, 1989). Managers reflect upon and begin to doubt their belief systems and personal values, particularly when the leader expresses negative judgment about the employee's actions.

When leaders attempt to gain acceptance of their ideas that are in conflict with associates' values, associates are often rendered powerless by the autocratic leader. The associate often rejects the leader's ideas and experiences them in direct conflict with their personal values. The conflict often becomes a source of psychological distress and self-doubt (Maier and Solem, 1952).

These four cases are among a larger set from Dr. Bogosian's silence research. In all cases, every research participant described a growing sense of self-doubt. They began to second-guess themselves and question their ability, significance, and self-worth. This self-doubt disrupted their ability to contribute to the organization with confidence.

Feelings of fear or futility play a central role in an employee's decision to remain silent[4]. Technically, this sort of circumstance is called

---

4   (Morrison & Rothman, 2009)

"Procedural Injustice" (Tyler, 1989). It's characterized as denied voice and denied decision control, and it breeds resentment against those who are "blameworthy" (p.103). The abusive leadership behavior that instills fear "most commonly occurs in the form of public ridicule, angry outbursts, taking credit for subordinates success, and scapegoating" (p. 262). Abused subordinates report greater levels of psychological distress and intentions to quit their jobs (Tepper & Lockhart, 2007). The consequences of leader inaction can lead to employees feeling a sense of futility. This then leads to a culture of silence. Consider how futility led to a culture of silence in the case below:

A chemist at a state crime laboratory allegedly altered test results tainting the reliability of evidence leading to convictions and jailing of thousands of people. Several of her peers supposedly knew that something was amiss about her behaviors— she was processing three times the number of samples than her colleagues— yet chose not to approach management. Why? Because one of them had tried to communicate with management and had been rebuffed. Specifically, he was told that this was not his job — back off or else. Based on that rebuff experience, employees quickly learned that any attempt to communicate this type of important work-related information was futile. The result was employee silence.

Leader behaviors such as those described in these cases are antecedents to organizational cultures of silence that can be characterized by the belief that speaking up about work-related issues are both futile and dangerous (Morrison and Milliken, 2000).

STEPPING BACK

Now that you've seen both sides of the coin (silence and voice), it's time to turn the lens on yourself. Think of the "delivery" of leadership as a hierarchy of observable behaviors, values, and (underlying) beliefs, as shown in Diagram 1.0. We believe that sustainable behavior change is unlikely without careful self-reflection and insights at each of three levels in the hierarchy shown below. As you read the next section, consider your own values and underlying beliefs and how your employees may experience them at work.

Diagram 1.0 The Delivery of Leadership

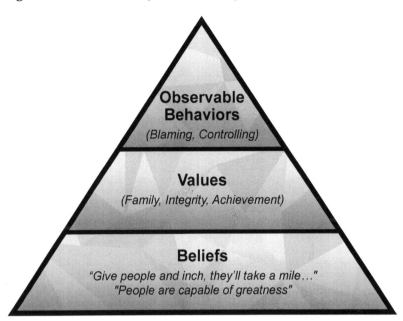

Your belief system explains how you see the world and what you believe to be true about it. Your belief system drives your values, which are the basis for your observable behaviors. Your behaviors impact how your associates experience you at work. Over time, if other leaders share your belief system and management style, you will begin to put in place a web of organizational symbols that reflect and bolster your beliefs and your style.

For example, take "control" as a behavior. High control is said to decrease the acceptance and openness to opposing or alternate views. It is also proposed that tall hierarchies put distance between management and employees that can foster beliefs among management that employees are unreliable and untrustworthy. If you believe that giving employees an inch means they will most likely take a mile, you are probably inclined to behave in ways that reflect this belief. This belief is manifested in espoused values of structure, control, and accountability. Living these values will be manifested in observable behaviors that represent your values and underlying beliefs such as the need to see frequent daily activities like status reports and daily update meetings.

Status reports may become an organizational symbol that reinforces the culture in your workplace.

The issue isn't whether status reports are good or bad. The issue is the underlying belief that drives your need for status reports and frequent check-ins with your associates. This belief, if unchecked, can drive behaviors that have undesirable and or unanticipated consequences for your employees—like feeling micro-managed.

Consider: A senior-level manager in a global manufacturer we interviewed in the course of this research explained that after several coaching meetings, she had begun to understand the root cause of her need to drive results and control all production projects closely and how to achieve a more balanced approach to her leadership. As a result, within a few weeks (weeks!), her employees began to speak up more than they had in the past, and overall, productivity was improving at a faster pace than before.

On the surface, driving results and controlling projects seemed like part of her job. However, her employees were burning out and resentful of the lack of autonomy and overt micromanagement. This leader discovered that her beliefs, values, and behaviors actually stemmed from being the oldest child growing up in a household of dysfunctional parents. The responsibility for her siblings rested on her shoulders, and she worked very hard to keep everything together for them. She learned at a young age that control was her saving grace, and it kept her siblings safe. She brought that perspective to work.

As soon as she understood the root cause of her controlling behavior, however, she felt free to explore ways to separate the behaviors that worked in the past from those in her current work life that had become a potential liability.

If you value structure and control, and your employees crave that direction, so much the better. But if you value structure and control, and your employees are motivated by autonomy, those two values, left unchecked and unexamined, could create tension and unresolved conflict. You can alter your behaviors when and if you receive feedback from those with whom you work. But you are unlikely to receive feedback if you have fostered a culture of silence, however unwittingly.

Now that you have read about several manager-employee interactions and their unintended consequences, you should have a sense of how cultures of silence are created. We now explore the concept of High-Influence Leadership®. We consider High-Influence Leadership® practices to be the antidote to leadership behaviors that may cause cultures of silence.

HIGH-INFLUENCE LEADERSHIP®

A High-Influence Leader is one who: (1) constantly learns and involves followers in the quest for excellence on an individual level and an organizational level (competitive superiority), (2) believes that followers have something to contribute, (3) encourages followers to learn and grow in their current role and beyond, (4) creates a level playing field for the purposes of innovating, gaining, and sustaining competitive advantage, and (5) encourages voice and minimizes silence in the workplace.

Research studies suggest that leaders often attribute poor performance to associates, and associates often attribute performance problems to their company and their leaders (Weiner, 1986). In addition, studies suggest that leaders often make attributions that maximize their (own) rewards and outcomes (Dossett & Greenberg, 1981). These attribution dynamics suggest that leaders and followers tend to self-protect. Self-protection mechanisms can lead to misunderstood motives that can result in a culture of silence.

High-Influence Leaders (HIL), on the other hand, think differently. When they experience an undesirable result at work, they ask themselves, "What part did I play in that result?" They hesitate to attribute negative results to others, and they avoid self-serving biases. High-Influence Leaders have a curious versus confirming learning orientation— they ask and listen more than they tell. They believe that most people are capable of succeeding, seek out and reward minority viewpoints, stimulate thinking rather than shut it down, and self-reflect and view feedback as a gift rather than a threat. As you think about the characteristics of the High-Influence Leader, consider the two following cases.

Ken is the CEO of a successful, New England-based investment company. A seasoned investment executive, he is constantly in tune with his influence on every aspect of the business.

"The [outside] investment world in which we operate is volatile. We are experts in our field. However, sometimes conflict is pushed to the limit due to outside pressures. We must remain calm, level-headed, and avoid over-reacting to current market conditions. This means that everyone involved in the business, whether Investments or Marketing and Sales, must have a voice and be willing to listen to others involved, even when their views are different. This is a major part of my role. I see myself as the neutralizer, the person who has to ensure that everyone is heard whether we like what we hear or not. I can't possibly have all the answers, and I don't. I work very hard at being accessible. I'm on the floor every chance I get so people have a chance to interact with me and vice versa. We are all on the same team, and we all play a big part in the company's success. If I don't set the example for a culture of voice and entrepreneurialism, who will?"

Bill, former COO emeritus of a major food manufacturer, was most proud of his company's record on recognition. According to Bill, this was the most important driver of the company's employee commitment.

"In a production environment, senior management must be seen as part of, not separate from, the line workers. I used to regularly walk the production facility and actually work on the line. No one in the company was more important than anyone else. I didn't think there was a better way for folks to connect with me and feel like they could have a voice. We were not big on hierarchical decision making, and we actually worked hard to decentralize it. We wanted upward communication, and we felt the best way to get that dynamic was to have the right leaders encouraging voice upward in the hierarchy."

These two leaders exemplify characteristics of a High-Influence Leader. They value humility and accessibility as methods of encouraging voice. Along with voice, they respect and believe in the contributions of others and see it as an asset to be treasured. In addition, both leaders believed that (appropriate) autonomy is a key success factor of their organizations.

Leaders have the ability to encourage levels of autonomy among their employee base or create levels of dependency (see diagram 1.1 below). The HIL enables appropriate levels of autonomy. They generally believe that employees are capable and can achieve success with coaching (not punishing), support, guidance, and feedback, assuming that employees are correctly placed in their roles and have the necessary resources to complete the job. The HIL encourages the well-placed employee to succeed, and when appropriate, provides decision-making latitude. The low influence leader may create a cycle of dependency when they micromanage or take back work at particular times prior to completion. If this take-back behavior becomes a pattern, employees quickly realize that they should only take tasks to a certain point, at which time they should hand the unfinished task back to the leader. The leader may assume the employee doesn't have initiative. The employee assumes that the leader wants it their way only and stops the process when they think they cannot or should not go further. Soon, there is a cycle of dependency that can lead to false, self-serving attribution by the leader. The diagram below illustrates both dependency and autonomy characteristics.

Diagram 1.1: The Dependency-Autonomy Continuum

Importantly, when we talk about "autonomy" and "dependency" here, we're not at all talking about the strict and completely necessary protocols that some companies must work under. Biotech firms, or organizations that investigate criminal activities, for example, have to follow strict protocols and processes to meet regulatory requirements, and/or to ensure safety. However, these companies can also have healthy cultures of voice. In fact, without cultures of voice, they are often at greater risk of a serious crisis.

Now that you have a better understanding of the primary causes of employee silence, it's time to reflect on the extent to which you may be creating a culture of voice or silence. In the next chapter, we'll describe a few ways to self-reflect; the exercises will help you understand your role in breaking corporate silence.

CHAPTER TWO
ANALYZE THE WAKE YOU CREATE

The term "wake" has numerous associations. Here, we're focusing on the pattern that is left by a moving object. A wake in this sense can be used as a jump point for leaders to propel themselves and the organization forward. Your beliefs, values, and behaviors result in what we call "The Wake." It is essentially the impact you have on others. These three elements build on one another to foster cultures of voice, and cultures of silence. In hindsight, it's easy to see how. But it's often difficult for leaders and managers to figure out what sort of culture they are perpetuating in real time or the wake they create.

That's because a person's own beliefs, values, and behaviors can be hard to assess objectively. The straightforward "look in the mirror" doesn't often reveal anything beyond justifiable mindsets and practices, particularly if the leader has the best interests of the organization at heart. (And you wouldn't be reading this book if you didn't.)

It's also hard to gain an objective perspective on your surroundings—literally, the infrastructure and tangibles that make up the climate in which you work. In Chapter One, we said that certain symbols—such as managers' lunchrooms, special parking spaces, or even regularly scheduled managers-only offsite retreats—can signal the kind of separation between employee and manager that may support a culture of silence. But that's not necessarily true in all cases. Some organizations with all of those symbolic bells and whistles have healthy cultures of voice. And many companies that tout their communal kitchens and the like in fact support crippling cultures of silence.

It's also easy to mistake a necessary protocol or a strict process for a "symbol" that would support a culture of silence—and, by contrast, to believe that if your organization doesn't have such strict protocols or processes, it has a culture of voice by default. Hospitals, biotech companies, food service companies, and manufacturing organizations of all kinds have very strict processes and often have highly defined and controlled communications channels. That doesn't mean that these organizations support cultures of silence.

Similarly, organizations that talk a great game of collaboration and equality, work-life balance, and being "green" can be concealing cultures of silence that permeate right from the front door to the president's desk—even if that desk isn't in a corner, and the president has just participated in a three-legged race down the hall with the receptionist to raise money for charity.

So, with all of these dire warnings on the table, how can you tell if yours is a culture of silence or a culture of voice, and to what extent it is one or the other?

The following three tools should help you start. The first tool is a three-part self-assessment for you to complete, focusing on:

- Your leadership mindset (beliefs and values)
- Your behaviors
- Organizational symbolism

The second tool is a survey for your employees to complete anonymously to help determine their engagement level. The third tool is a "Try It and Track It®" exercise that will offer you a few specific tactics to take with an eye toward monitoring the changes (if any) you see in the behaviors of those around you as a result. By doing so, you'll be able to see how much you can—and possibly should—be trying to change the culture at your organization.

CULTURE OF SILENCE, CULTURE OF VOICE ASSESSMENTS
TOOL #1-SELF-ASSESSMENT

PART I: SELF-ASSESSMENT

Answer the following questions related to your *Leadership Mindset (beliefs and values)*:

1. **What percentage of meetings have you attended in the last one or two months where agreement was reached quicker than the time you thought it would require?**

    - How did meeting participants respond?
    - What was the outcome?

    Reaching agreement too quickly can be an indication that not all viewpoints were heard or solicited. The time it takes to reach agreement depends on several variables, like the number of participants from whom agreement is sought, the content complexity, time constraints, and level of risk. For example, it takes less time to get agreement on the new break-room paint color than it takes to get agreement to change an archaic business process.

    If you answer more than 50% to this question, you may need to reflect on the influence practices used in the agreement process. If you are the owner of the outcome, try NOT to express your views until at least three others have been able to express theirs without judgment.

2. **How many employees, in the last month, presented a solution to a problem when you didn't have a solution to offer?**

    - What was your response?
    - What was their response?

If you answer "zero" to this question, it may indicate a need to actively solicit more views and opinions from others as a regular part of your solution process. If, upon reflection, you realize that your employees often wait for you to provide the answer, you probably need to start involving others in the innovation (idea generation) process. When others present ideas to you, you should always acknowledge theirs and clearly explain the idea selection criteria. Doing so reduces speculation, which is often wrong, about the decision making process. Trouble begins when employees start to socialize their speculation (with colleagues). Suddenly, *"My way or the highway,"* or the equivalent, becomes part of your leadership brand.

3. **In how many staff meetings, within the last six months, did you get the "bovine stare"—a blank look—from the group when you asked people to give you their opinions?**

    - What was your response?
    - What was their response?

If your answer is greater than 1, it may indicate a dependence on your viewpoint, your decision making, and employee disengagement. Don't assume that silence means agreement—it rarely does. To intervene when this happens next, ask for other views and ideas, and immediately start counting (silently). We doubt that you will count as high as 45 seconds because the silence will be intolerable and someone will speak up.

PART II: SELF-ASSESSMENT

Answer the following questions related to *Behavior*:

4. **Who were the employees, within the last week, to call you or show up at your office (unsolicited) with a new idea?**

    - What was your response?
    - What was their response?

If there were none, it may indicate an unwillingness to interact with you. It could also mean that your employees are very busy, autonomous, and have no need to interact with you. In either case, start to reflect on the individual and group interactions you have with your employees. You may be inadvertently sending messages that say, *"Stay away,"* vs. *"Welcome."*

5. **Within the last week, who were the employees that openly disagreed with you?**

   - What was your response?
   - What was their response?

If there were none, it may indicate that disagreement with you, the leader, is not permissible and has negative consequences. Negative consequences are defined by your employees, not you, and they are based on your past performance when handling disagreements.

If you have ever openly disagreed with an employee in a group setting that was experienced by them as "uncomfortable" or "disparaging," others are unlikely to put themselves in harm's way. Start to reflect on both your verbal and non-verbal communication when you disagree with employees. Chapter 5 has specific self-reflection and insights recommendations that you can apply to verbal and non-verbal communication.

6. **How many employees, within the last month, presented information related to change that sounded like resistance?**

   - What was your response?
   - What was their response?

If your initial reaction is "too many," it may indicate an unwillingness to listen to the views and opinions of others in change situations where you have a large stake in the outcome. When change occurs, it often has emotional repercussions among the employee population. Their reactions may be an attempt to make sense of the change, and they should have a safe place (without judgment) to do that with you. Their expressed concerns may contain valuable information that can inform the change process. When you think you are hearing "resistance," shift your thinking to, *"This could be valuable information."*

7. **How many half-baked ideas have you received from employees in the last two weeks that you hope will die on the vine?**

   - What was your response?
   - What was their response?

If it feels like there were "too many," it may indicate that you are not building up the half-baked ideas enough. Building up half-baked ideas involves saying what you like about the idea first. Then state your concerns in the form of questions to encourage and teach the employee where and how they can improve the idea.

8. **How many times in the last month have you responded to an employee idea with the phrase, "Let me play Devil's Advocate?" or something equivalent?**

   - What was their response?
   - What was their response?

If you answer "a few" or more, it may indicate an overreliance on this feedback method. "Devil's Advocate" may work with some of your employees, especially if the relationship is safe and secure. Don't assume that it can work with all of them. There are probably those with whom this is the wrong method. It can promote defensiveness and increase the employee's dependency on your ideas and decisions. Alternatively, try using a more encouraging feedback method than "Devil's Advocate." We offer some suggestions in Chapter Three.

PART III: SELF-ASSESSMENT

Answer the following questions related to *Organizational Symbolism* (bearing in mind that there are no "right" or "wrong" answers and that symbolism does not necessarily indicate one type of culture or another):

9. **How many executive parking spaces are there at the office building where you work?**

If you answer more than zero, there may be a sense of injustice among the employee population. Special treatment is an invitation to organizational justice evaluation. *Organizational Justice*[5] is the employee's sense of how they are treated. Special parking spaces may be symbols of injustice that can result in decreased trust, decreased employee commitment, and increased conflict.

10. Is there a separate executive dining room?
(If "yes," see #9 above)

11. What is the dress code in your organization?

- Does it change by function and department? Why?
- How many leaders in the C-Suite wear jackets and ties when they enter your workspace?

If the management population looks (overall appearance, clothing, accessories) very different compared to everyone else, employees often perceive the difference as a reason to distance themselves from those in other groups, like the C-Suite members. There are obvious differences in this case, and when employees see that the management culture looks differently, talks differently, and acts differently, they can conclude that members of that group have *"no interest in what I (employee) have to say,"* resulting in a culture of silence.

12. How many times, in the last two months, has an Executive Team Member (CEO, CIO, CFO) had a casual conversation with one of your employees?

If you answer "never or very few," it may indicate an issue of isolation. Employees want to know that they matter to those in charge, that their membership in the organization is important, and that they are significant. Senior team isolation may cause employees to speculate about it. When speculation rises, so does anxiety. Senior team members should be visible in the employee culture whenever and wherever possible. If you are a senior management member, try to eat lunch in the employee cafeteria once per week, sit with people, and introduce yourself. Ask how they are doing. Ask what they think about a relevant

---

5   Cropanzano, Bowen & Gilliland, 2007

issue happening in the organization. This interaction can affirm an employee's sense of significance, belonging, and self-esteem[6].

The questions above are designed to encourage self-reflection. Cultures of silence are constructed one employee at a time. One "unintended behavior" on the part of a leader can contribute more than you know to supporting a culture of silence—employees may not talk to you, but word will spread among them. And the 15th person to hear that you cut someone off when they were trying to talk —say, by putting a hand up in their face — is NOT going to come back to you and ask, *"What was that all about?"* The rate and seriousness of the "rumor mill" has to do with your prior behaviors and the extent to which you are able to determine whether your actions might be misinterpreted. Say, for example, you put your hand up to silence someone. Maybe that person is constantly interrupting. Maybe you had an off day. Either way, that gesture sends a message to others that it is too risky to give input. They may respond with the "bovine stare."

This three part self–assessment provides you with insight into your beliefs, values, behaviors, and organizational symbols. The next tool relates to the experiences of your employees and the cultural consequences.

CULTURE OF SILENCE, CULTURE OF VOICE ASSESSMENTS
TOOL #2-ANONYMOUS EMPLOYEE SURVEY

EMPLOYEE SURVEY

The purpose of this survey (below) is to assess a culture of silence. If you attempt to conduct a survey, it is critical that your employees are confident in their anonymity. If they are not, this survey may not be worth doing. So, if your department is fairly small, do not make your employees identify their job title or level. They will sense whether you will be able to figure out who wrote what, and they may tailor their answers to conceal their identity.

---

6   Maslow, A. H. 1954

In fact, if yours is a small department (fewer than seven people), a better approach might be to skip the survey in favor of hiring an objective and trustworthy third-party consultant to conduct a "listening tour" and ask employees to discuss their department, division, and company experiences. In smaller organizations, employees may consider human resource staff to be encumbered by the current culture, and they may again alter their answers accordingly.

EMPLOYEE SURVEY:[7]

Instructions: Answer the questions below with either (A) to indicate *Always*, (S) to indicate *Sometimes*, (N) to indicate *Never*.

Employee Survey

1. It is risky for me to speak up to management if I think something is wrong.

2. It is risky for me to share relevant information with our management.

3. It is safer for me (my general well being at work, and my employment status) to omit pertinent facts about work-related problems than to disclose them.

4. It is best for me NOT to express ideas for improvements because doing that can get you in trouble if they think my idea is wrong.

5. I have ideas for change and improvement, and my colleagues probably do, too, but we don't share those ideas with each other, or with management.

6. There is a general unwillingness among my colleagues to speak up with suggestions for change.

7. It is futile for any of my peers to offer ideas to management.

8. I think my colleagues and I feel that it is safer to keep ideas about change or solutions to ourselves.

9. It seldom makes a difference to suggest ideas for improvement.

10. My colleagues and I talk about solutions and change among ourselves, but we don't bring those ideas to management.

---

7   Adapted from Van Dyne, L. 1999. Used with permission

If your employees answered (A) *Always* or (S) *Sometimes* to just three of these questions, you may be working in a culture of silence. Your employees may be withholding important work-related information based on the "unwritten rules" or "established norms" of your work place. The trouble is, of course, that the employee culture will rarely inform the management culture of its established norms.

Think back again to the "bovine stare" question in your own self-assessment. It's the end of a meeting and you ask, "O.K., does anyone have any comments or suggestions about X?" Your employees look at you blankly and wait until you say, "O.K., then, we're all good."

But are you? Your employees are unlikely to provide you with a reason for the collective "stare." Don't expect them to give you any clues into their behavior. They will discuss and collude with each other but not with you. It's likely that you are perceived as being a member of the "management" clique, which is separate and distinct from the "employee group." The "employee group," in a culture of silence, has one major concern: how it will survive and prosper under your leadership. Determining its survival means that it watches everything you do and say to figure you out, and it responds in a way that best protects its survival.

It is your responsibility to detect a culture of silence, reflect on your leadership practices, and watch your associates' behavior and interactions with you to determine how to move toward a culture a voice. This idea leads us to the third exercise, and your first opportunity to try some new tactics and see what happens.

CULTURE OF SILENCE, CULTURE OF VOICE ASSESSMENTS
TOOL #3-SELF-ASSESSMENT

TRY IT AND TRACK IT® EXERCISE

So far, we have given you two diagnostic tools—one, a reflective self-assessment, and another, an employee survey to test the presence and strength of a culture of silence. Drawing specifically on the employee survey, but also being mindful of the results of your self-assessment, it's time to try several tactical practices and then track what happens as a direct outcome of each practice.

If you have a culture of silence in your organization, these practices should show you how small changes in your behavior can have significant ripple effects that can help move to a culture of voice. You may not be able to change an organization-wide culture of silence single-handedly, but you can certainly influence the micro-culture in your business area immediately and positively.

If you have a culture of voice, these practices will reinforce it, and help you become purposeful about avoiding a culture of silence. Small changes in your behavior can make a big difference in the organizational culture.

There are eight *Signals of Silence*®. Using the table below, start by considering the *Signals of Silence* in Column One. Based on the results of your employee survey, which of these signals concern you most? Pick one, and then consider the *Leadership Practice*, in Column Two, that encourages voice. Then use the *Try and Track It*® routine (in Column Three) to try the practice and monitor the results.

Table 2.1: Try It and Track It ® Table

Signals of Silence	Practices that Encourage Voice	Try It & Track It®
1. Employees appear unwilling to speak up with suggestions for change.	Ask your direct reports in a small group (small groups can encourage more interaction that large ones) of not more than 5-8 people: Ask, *"If you could change one thing that we do right now, what would it be"*? Ask each of them to respond. Wait 45 seconds without speaking. But if you get the *"bovine stare"*, ask them to write down their thoughts and then facilitate a discussion about what was written.	• What specifically did you do (differently)? • What was the result? • What did you learn about yourself?
2. Employees have indicated that it is futile to offer ideas to management.	When a suggestion is made and not implemented, go back to the originator. Explain what you liked about their idea, the decision-making criteria and the reason for the outcome. Strongly encourage and explicitly seek that person's input again.	• What specifically did you do (differently)? • What was the result? • What did you learn about yourself?
3. Employees believe that it is safer to keep ideas about solutions to oneself.	When you hear an idea that seems half-baked, use build-up language to get to a better solution. For example, ask: How will you handle (concerns)...? Never tear down the idea or criticize it especially in a public setting.	• What specifically did you do (differently)? • What was the result? • What did you learn about yourself?

Signals of Silence	Practices that Encourage Voice	Try It & Track It®
4. Employees feel that it seldom makes a difference to suggest ideas for improvement.	Periodically ask your associates for one thing in their control that could be improved. Listen without judgment.	• What specifically did you do (differently)? • What was the result? • What did you learn about yourself?
5. Employees believe that it is risky to speak up and suggest ideas for change with our management.	In your next staff meeting, ask your direct reports to write down 2-3 things that should be changed by senior management that would improve how things get done. Discuss the items and get an agreement on the 2-3 items that you can agree will be delivered to your boss for consideration. This is not a firm commitment, but a promise to give them a voice with your boss.	• What specifically did you do (differently)? • What was the result? • What did you learn about yourself?
6. Employees fear sharing even relevant information with our management.	Changing this practice requires a collective and encouraging leader response to information that is undesirable to hear. If in the moment, a leader colleague seems to be shooting the messenger, intervene if possible. Refocus the attention on the relevant information and express your gratitude to the messenger.	• What specifically did you do (differently)? • What was the result? • What did you learn about yourself?

Signals of Silence	Practices that Encourage Voice	Try It & Track It®
7. Employees believe it is safer to omit pertinent facts about work related problems than to disclose them.	The next time an associate discusses a problem, ask what they believe to be the cause? Ask "why" at least 3 times to increase the likelihood that you get to root cause. Listen without judgment.	• What specifically did you do (differently)? • What was the result? • What did you learn about yourself?
8. Employees worry that it is too risky to present solutions to our management.	The 'risk' associated with knowledge transfer is usually the result of witnessing or hearing of a colleague who suffered the consequences of presenting a solution upwards. Unfortunately, you may be guilty by association (with the management rank). Either way, you must combat this cultural reality by removing all risk responses, for example: • "That will never work" • "We already tried that" • "You may not understand" Simply listen without judgment.	• What specifically did you do (differently)? • What was the result? • What did you learn about yourself?

The eight Signals of Silence®, the corresponding Leadership Practices that encourage voice, and the Try It and Track It® method will help you to shape a culture of voice.

GOING ALONG TO GET ALONG

A culture of silence is exemplified by loss of confidence, loss of enthusiasm, and a sense of lost power. Employees feel inferior. They are unsure of how to communicate – what words to choose, what methods to use. They do not feel respected, and they worry that if they do extend themselves—if they do want to contribute discretionary effort— their effort will be rebuffed because it will violate the organization's established norms. They just go along to get along rather than feel any humiliation. Discretionary Effort[8] is the extra effort (for example, extra hours and going above and beyond what is expected to help achieve organizational goals) that employees extend beyond what they know to be the minimal requirements to sustain their current work role. Our research indicates that Discretionary Effort can be elastic. It can expand when employees experience a sense of justice and fairness or contract when employees experience a sense of injustice or egregious leadership practices. Research[9] indicates that employees can alter the quality and quantity of their work to restore justice when they perceive that there is an injustice. Discretionary effort can also affect employee engagement.

Organizations that have a culture of silence are characterized by a lack of employee engagement. A lack of engagement manifests itself with a lack of (emotional) connection, motivation, dialogue, candor, risk–taking, and knowledge transfer. Employees become defensive due to their sense of "injustice." Feelings of anger and frustration can heighten yet remain hidden. In the organizations we've studied, we have observed employee dissatisfaction "brewing," and even pockets of rebellion characterized by subtle sabotage. And subtle sabotage often takes place on an unconscious and almost unobservable level. It can be more harmful than overt sabotage, which can be identified and confronted. Employees are more inclined to go along to get along.

---

8   Lloyd, R. (2008)

9   Wang, X., et al. (2010).

CONTRIBUTING FULLY, WILLFULLY

A culture of voice, by contrast, is exemplified by employees' desire and ability to participate in discussions, disagreements, and decision making. It is the interaction-fostering contribution of intentions, ideas, and information. It is the ability to be involved, to choose to involve oneself, and to have meaningful connections.

A culture of voice is likely to result in employee perceptions of fairness, realization of intrinsic opportunities, tangible and visible extrinsic opportunities, and self-efficacy. Employees believe that they can attain their goals, that they have the right and opportunity to speak about what they think and feel, that news, both good and bad will be shared, that they feel valued and significant, and that their manager will forgive mistakes because the "experience" is valued! Lastly, a culture of voice is likely to result in an emotional commitment[10] to work and to others at work.

In a culture of voice, employees take smart risks and make sound decisions. They are empowered to use their skills, knowledge, intelligence, and talents to the fullest.

THE WAKE YOU CREATE

Your beliefs, values, and behaviors create your "wake." The wake you create can either elicit silence or encourage voice. In hindsight, it's easy to see how. But it's often difficult for leaders and managers to step back and analyze the wake they create. You now have several diagnostic tools (self-assessment, employee survey questions, Try It and Track It method) to self-reflect and gain insight into the wake you create. What have you discovered about your wake? How can you adjust your wake even further, as needed, to encourage voice and minimize silence in the workplace?

In our work with leaders and managers, we've repeatedly been asked to "get the employees engaged." We've heard: "I want them to use their potential." "I want them motivated. I need them to ..."

---

10   Slap, S. (2010).

A more productive line of questioning would be, "How can I help my employees engage? How can I help them use their potential? How can I better understand what motivates them so that I provide the best available opportunities for them to learn and grow in their current roles and beyond (if appropriate)?"

In this turbulent, rapidly changing world, many U.S. corporations are over-managed and under-led. That is, leaders focus on the "what" but not the "why" nor the true needs of the "who." In aiming for peak measurable results, they ignore the foundation of engagement.

In the next chapter, we will start examining ways in which you can become a High-Influence Leader and purposefully create the foundation for a healthy culture of voice.

CHAPTER THREE
SIX LEADERSHIP PRACTICES THAT HELP CREATE A CULTURE OF VOICE

You're now equipped with an understanding of what a culture of silence is and a sense of whether (and how much) it may affect the organization you help manage. That means you can start to work purposefully to encourage a culture of voice.

To be a little more exact, you can now focus on encouraging voice with two distinct but interdependent goals: 1) Encouraging voice—resulting in employee willingness to speak up, speak out, and expand discretionary effort; and 2) Your own ability to hear what they're saying and use that information for the good of the company. Making discernable progress towards those goals will improve the way in which people throughout your organization relate to one another, to their leaders, and to the people they lead.

You've probably heard the idea that in order to encourage a certain type of behavior, you have to model it. We believe that advice. We're not suggesting, however, that there is one size that fits all for instilling a culture of voice throughout your company. No two managers are alike, nor should they be. You can have a vastly different style of managing from the manager in the next department or the organization that rents the space next to yours, and all three of you may foster strong cultures of voice in which expanded discretionary effort is the norm, not the exception.

That's why, in this chapter, we describe six leadership practices that encourage employee voice. As you read, we recommend that you take in the big picture, but don't feel as if there is one right way to act on any of the practices we're recommending. Instead, consider each practice against the way you learn best and your natural style. Remember, you can encourage a culture of voice whether you're a loud speaker or a soft speaker, and whether you're an introvert or an extrovert. And you can encourage a culture of voice whether your organization must adhere to strict protocols or not. Cultures of voice can flourish in highly regulated environments. Cultures of silence can (sadly) flourish even in open-concept "flat" organizations with enviable benefits!

The six leadership practices are:

1. Maximize Your Emotional Intelligence
2. Strengthen Your Resilience
3. Learn More Than You Affirm
4. Ask More Than You Tell
5. Strengthen versus Discount
6. Coach versus Punish

We'll talk about each one in turn.

PRACTICE #1: MAXIMIZE YOUR EMOTIONAL INTELLIGENCE

Emotional Intelligence (EI) is the ability to sense, understand, manage, and apply the power and information of your emotions as your greatest source of energy, influence, and connection. It is self-awareness and awareness of others in the moment. It is the ability to analyze your own emotions and analyze the emotions/feelings of others. It is the ability to pick up on subtle cues including tone of voice, eye contact, facial expression, and body language. It is picking up on others' emotions and responding appropriately. If you understand and name your own emotions, you can more readily pick up on the emotions of others.

Learning more about Emotional Intelligence will help you recognize gaps—gaps in communication, gaps between your intentions and behaviors, gaps in what you perceive to be engagement versus what is reality. With a higher EI, you'll know yourself better. You will hone your ability to recognize your "default" reactions, respect yourself, and respond appropriately to yourself. And as you do so, you'll be in a better position to recognize, respect, and respond appropriately to others.

You are not responsible for the feelings of another. But as a leader, you are responsible for creating an environment where others are able to choose their own emotional state. Also note that people feel before they think. And how they feel impacts how they act.

Consider the employees at one hotel in Connecticut. Christine was there during one leg of a business trip and had some time to work on this book. As she put it:

"I took a break for breakfast. And I found that the breakfast crew was completely engaged, with me, with the other guests, and with one another. They were upbeat; they went out of their way to assist me. I told them I was spending the day working on a book related to employee engagement. They told me I should spend the day with them because all of them, every employee, were fully engaged. I took the bait, and I spent the next few hours going around the hotel, taking a poll. I was astonished to learn that they all, as promised, seemed fully engaged! Here are some of the answers I got when I asked 'Why?'":

"We are appreciated. We get acknowledgements of our efforts."

"We are not micro-managed. This boosts our morale immensely. We are actually free to make mistakes. We do get told about the mistakes, are asked for correction ideas, and then the mistake is forgotten."

"We are a team. It feels like a great team here. Our managers jump in to help. They let us know that they are not better than us. They don't take over our work, but we know by the way that they're willing to pitch in that we all have the same goal—to create a very positive experience for our guests."

"We feel like our suggestions are valuable to them."

"Our managers listen to us. They always make us feel as if they have time. And if they're pressed for time right in the moment, they follow up with us later."

"Our managers like their jobs. They are happy, and it makes us happy. Their attitude is contagious."

"You get what you give. We know that, and they know that too."

"We know what they expect from us. It is very clear. That makes us comfortable to ask questions and to re-ask when we do not understand."

"Do you know, even if we are over-worked, and we are sometimes, it is okay because they appreciate it and let us know how much it means."

"I left a position at a competitor because I was never listened to. The only reason I had stayed was because the pay was better. But you reach a point when you need to be treated as an individual who has something to contribute. I felt I did not make a difference there. I make a difference here."

The managers at this hotel clearly have a high EI. It's also likely that *their* managers—regional, divisional—do too. They put the "who" before the "what," and it serves them well. As Sir Isaac Newton wrote, "Men build too many walls and not enough bridges." He was right.

PRACTICE #2: STRENGTHEN YOUR RESILIENCE

It's easy to assume that an organization has a culture of voice when times are good. In fact, it's easier to have a culture of voice when times are good. But what about when times are turbulent or downright difficult? (In other words, a lot of the time for a lot of companies these days!)

44

When associates are stressed, when they feel as if they cannot cope, they are prone to behavioral changes — losing their voice and losing a desire to engage. How will they be changed by difficult times, disappointment, and adversity? Will the behavioral changes in them be intentional or will they be random reactions with little sustainable merit? They may lapse into silence and for sure will lose engagement. How will you use the difficult experience to further assist them in discovering their uniqueness, enhancing their resolve, revealing and using untapped potential, and strengthening relationships? How will you help them remain engaged? How will you create an environment that encourages them to have a voice?

We recommend using the following behaviors during difficult times as stepping-stones to strengthen your resilience:

Feel Your Feelings Through. Take the time to understand what your experience really is and what emotions you're feeling. When dealing with adversity, people often feel some combination of shock, anger, disbelief, jealousy, sadness, and loss. You may feel victimized, incapacitated, and even stupid. Listen to what is going on inside of you. Be brutally honest with yourself. Write down your emotions. Then think about what's behind each one. Doing so may help you set a deliberate course of action to mitigate each negative emotional response and then help others recognize what they're feeling.

Choose Your Frame of Reference. Your subconscious mind is extremely powerful, so be careful of what you feed it. A negative outlook may cause you to feel defeated and de-energized before you even start to act. If your *self-talk* is consistently negative, you'll be painting yourself as a victim. People tend to attract and become that which they think about. Be purposeful about holding yourself in good regard despite what may be happening around you. As a manager in a struggling or even sinking company, this can be so hard to do, but the effort to focus on a positive and realistic frame of reference—*"Given the situation, what can we do that represents a step forward?"*—will serve you and your organization well.

Simplify. What are the essentials at work and at home? What can you say *"No"* to right now to focus on what matters most? What can your employees pare away in order to concentrate on critical activities? Return to the basics. Write down your values and your priorities, and commit to honoring them. What are your priorities?

Balance. Remember that there is a life outside of the turbulence at work, and pay attention to your own health and habits. Don't sacrifice your health and wellbeing for the company; it won't work for the company or for you.

Advise Yourself as You Would Advise Another. Act as your own coach. What would you advise someone in your situation to do? Do not aim for perfection or for a perfect resolution. Set viable goals.

PRACTICE #3: LEARN MORE THAN YOU AFFIRM

This practice refers to your learning orientation—learner (curious) or judge (affirming). Let's say you're in a staff meeting to discuss a problem and the solution to it. You've seen this type of problem before, but you want to bring the troops together to get everyone on board. So, you present the problem, how you see it, and proceed to offer your solution. Then, in the final act to secure commitment and to be sure you hear others, you ask, "Does everyone agree?" Surely someone will offer a contrary view if they have one because this is a smart group who tends to be vocal. Well, think again.

If your problem-solving methodology is to offer the solution first and then solicit contrary views, you can count on a typical response that we refer to as the bovine stare. (We're not sure if this is similar to the "GM Nod" but it sure sounds as if the two might be related.) The bovine stare is characterized by a blank look on your associates' faces as they either stare off in the distance or down at the agenda (if there is one) until you say—usually after your silence time threshold is crossed, which is probably about 10 seconds—*"Okay, then I guess we all agree."*

Big Mistake! If your organization has even a tinge of a culture of silence, who is going to dare to offer you, the checkbook holder, a contrary view, especially when you seem so confident in the path forward?

Research suggests—not surprisingly—that managers react unfavorably when employees offer contrary views that they perceive as a threat (Burris & Deter, 2012). So, who is going to risk that reaction, especially if they feel they're going out on a limb to do so? After all, the solution, your rendition of it, has already been presented, and because of the power you hold, it may be too risky to present a contrary view, especially if it is in the minority.

What is the antidote? To answer this question, we must explore your learning orientation.

A learning orientation refers to an underlying belief about your role as the leader of the problem-solving process and knowledge-transfer agent. Are you a judge (affirming your views and opinions) or a learner (curious to learn about other views and opinions)? Consider the two opposites and the characteristics of each on a continuum depicted in the diagram (3.0) below.

Diagram 3.0: Learning Orientation

Manager as Judge *(affirming)*	**Manager as Learner** *(curious)*

• Affirming Orientation	• Curiosity Orientation
• Decision Maker	• Decision Process Facilitator
• "I should know everything"	• "I have everything to know"

First, consider the example of the manager as the judge with an affirming learning orientation:

The judge believes that along with the position of authority comes inherent knowledge and wisdom. When problems surface, this type of leader believes that she is *supposed to have the answers*—after all, that's why she is in her position of power and authority. This mindset puts tremendous pressure on the leader—and it is flawed thinking! But it is not uncommon. The consequence of the judge mindset is the behavior it can create among your employees. If you, the power-holder, establish a central decision-making and problem-solving norm, you will essentially train your staff to acquiesce to your actions and views. This encourages a culture of silence. After a while, why *would* most staff members speak up and voice their opinions when it's usually yours that is used in the end? Without intending to, you've caused them to think that voicing their views is futile.

What's more, your staff will spend endless amounts of energy trying to figure out what you want and how *you* would solve problems versus how *they* would solve problems. In the process, they may cease to pay attention to their own instincts, knowledge, and thinking. Is this your intent?

In the example above, the manager (you) got compliance but not commitment or energy. Most subordinates will now go through the motions of your solution but without conviction. They may do what you've told them to do even if they know that your solution won't solve the problem. In the world of process and productivity analysis, this is called "waste."

Consider a different type of example, the manager as learner, with a curious learning orientation:

The business unit Executive Vice President (EVP) in a global wholesale organization opens the meeting this way: "Our challenge is to figure out how to integrate the two company cultures. Let's get some process suggestions for gathering ideas to address this challenge. I'd like to be able to reach an agreement on the best two or three solutions to this challenge before we leave this meeting."

Now you're onto something. You're a great example of a High-Influence Leader with a (curious) learning orientation. You're curious about others' views and opinions, and you draw them out at every opportunity. You've established a solution process that encourages idea sharing and minority views in an attempt to reach the best possible solution, idea, and decision. The idea you end up with may be based on the one you propose, but we think it will be a "new and improved" version of what you were originally thinking. And even if it is exactly what you had in mind from the start, you can be confident that it has been vetted adequately.

PRACTICE #4: ASK MORE THAN YOU TELL

Basically, this influence practice is about spending more time asking questions than telling others what to do. We call this practice the 20/80 Rule. As a guideline, try to limit the amount of time you "tell" others to 20% of interaction time, and ask questions (inquire) to understand and learn 80% of the time. This may seem like a leader's paradox. After all, didn't you get to this level in your company by having the answers? Perhaps. However, this paradox is built on the myth that leaders actually have all the answers. Actually, the higher you rise on the corporate ladder, the more you may realize that you actually have more questions than answers.

Sometimes, when a leader still feels that he or she must have all the answers, we ask this obnoxious question: "Did you hire stupid people?" The leader will inevitably protest: "Of course not!" Well, then can't those smart people who work for you have some good answers sometimes? Doesn't it show you, as a leader, in a really good light if you have innovative, engaged people working for you—people who have ideas and sometimes answers?

Curiosity means that you are capable of learning. A strong learning orientation means that you are capable of growing and expanding your thinking. In a world that is constantly moving, changing, and disrupted by breakthrough technology, learning is essential for every leader and every business. Research[11] shows that companies that have a high-velocity learning capacity outperform their competitors. The companies capable of learning faster than their competitors will have a distinct advantage that can be measured by market value.

So, when you are sure you have heard someone clearly, unencumbered by your own thoughts and opinions, use your curiosity to draw them out and learn as much as you can about their views, opinions, solutions, and recommendations.

High-Influence Leaders use a practice known as focused listening to ask and learn more than tell, guide rather than judge, and encourage dialogue rather than shut it down. This doesn't mean that you don't get to insert views and opinions. It means that you build your understanding of an issue with the added insights you've gained from your associates' judgment, knowledge, ideas, and rationale. In this way, you are in a strong position to guide and direct—from a place of thorough understanding rather than a place of assumptions.

The term focused listening has been used way too often in business without an understanding of what it means. As a result, the meaning has been diluted. If you think you're familiar with it, please consider it anew. We think it matters a great deal in organizations where rapid knowledge transfer is a competitive advantage. Focused listening is actually a two-part practice that consists of passive listening and reflective listening (also sometimes called verifying). Together, these two parts will ensure that when people do speak up, you don't minimize, misdirect, or misunderstand what they're trying to tell you and why.

Let's deal with the toughest component of focused listening first: passive listening. Basically, it works like this: Shut up and listen! Really, that's it. But it's surprisingly hard to do because most of us have grown accustomed to constant and rapid stimuli such as email, text, and instant messaging. We don't know for how long to shut up. In fact, many of us are uncomfortable with silence. We wait until the speaker with whom we are interacting takes a breath of air so that we can jump in (verbally) to the conversation with our thoughts, views, and opinions.

---

11   Jimenez & Sanz-Ville, 2011

How long does it take between the time you first experience silence and the moment when you pick up your mobile device to check it for messages, send a message, or do something else with it? How long do you wait until the person with whom you are interacting makes their point and when you jump in with your view? What percentage of total concentration do you give your associates, colleagues, and clients during communication interactions?

Absolute concentration is physiologically difficult because your mind is capable of processing approximately 450 words per minute,[12] but people speak at an average of approximately 150 words per minute. So it's quite natural for your mind to speed along three times faster than anyone's physical ability to speak. This rapid mind processing is like an internal chatterbox.

Your internal chatterbox can be controlled when you focus on the speaker—whether in person, on the phone, in an email, or during text conversation. And we suggest you have a go at controlling it.

Try this out the next time someone knocks at your office door in need of your time. Simply push away all electronic devices, look at the person speaking, eye-to-eye, and LISTEN to them for one minute—60 seconds[13]. Do not interrupt; do not make hurry-up noises or gestures; do not nod as if you already know what they mean. Don't even offer an encouraging phrase, like, "Oh yes, go on." Just listen. After the 60 seconds are up, think about what you heard. Did you hear more or less than what you might have heard if you had allowed your internal chatterbox to remain at high volume?

Now we'll get into the second component of focused listening—reflective listening (or verifying).

Basically, reflective listening means checking to be sure you correctly grasped the essence of the speaker's message, verifying that your grasp is correct.

---

12   Nichols & Lewis, 1963

13   Huszczo, G. E. 1996

This task isn't as easy as it may seem because your associates may want to tell you more than you (think) you need or want to know. At times they can load up their conversations with extraneous and distracting information. Their emotions may also be causing them to add in tangential information. This makes focused listening tough, especially if your internal chatterbox is saying, "Get to the point!" But, you signed up for this leadership job, and when employees need your time, you are obligated to give it to them.

The best way to reflect back on what you heard is to acknowledge the two things that people will always do in communication interactions: 1) tell you what they think, and 2) show you how they feel. So, two critical reflection components are:

1. Acknowledge what was said—a summary is sufficient. Acknowledging says, "Here's what I heard from you," without any judgment. "Without judgment" doesn't mean you don't have any; it just means that you are deliberately "bracketing" your views so that you are free and clear to acknowledge what was said.

Bracketing[14] is the process of recognizing and setting aside your thoughts and views, which may get in the way of your associates' thoughts and views and cloud your response. Your job is to listen clearly, unencumbered by your internal chatterbox. Bracketing will help you to focus on your associates' current state of mind and how they view a problem, solution, or innovation.

2. Recognize the meaning of the speaker's intonation and body language. Research shows that the voice tone and body language expressed in any interaction where emotion plays a part accounts for 93 percent of a message (A. Mehrebian, UCLA). The actual spoken words only account for seven percent of a message communicated. So, in the vernacular: it's not what one says; it's how one says it that matters most to the message receiver.

---

14   Husserl, E. (1931)

PRACTICE #5: STRENGTHENING OTHERS VERSUS DISCOUNTING THEM

To understand what we mean by "strengthening," it's important to be able to recognize its opposite, "discounting." The term discounting signifies the perception of a message received from the message sender (1988, Weaver). Discounting includes both verbal and non-verbal communication practices perceived as put-downs. In other words, if you "discount" someone, that person can experience a threat to their self-esteem and sense of significance. Your associates will go to great lengths to protect their self-esteem and dignity, even if that means they withhold ideas that might be relevant toward a hoped-for innovation or a potentially important contribution to problem solving. Remember the "bovine stare?" If you're discounting, that's what you'll see.

According to Dr. Tim Weaver, a former Boston University Professor, discounting is so common in companies that we have all become immune to it. People often make excuses for their boss's discounting behaviors by explaining it away. For example, managers will often say, "This is just the way my boss communicates." Discounting within leader/subordinate relationships may be difficult to correct because of the inherent power disequilibrium in that relationship. How do you tell your boss that, 1) their communication style, at times, is discounting and has negative effects and 2) that it needs to change?

We asked thousands of middle- and senior-level leaders in 14 countries, High-Influence Leadership® program participants, to construct a list of verbal discounts that they have either said or that have been said to them. We also asked them to describe the feelings that the discount triggered. These are summarized in the table (3.1) below:

Table 3.1: Discounting Table

Discounting Table

Verbal Discount	Emotional Consequence
"That won't work"	I Felt devalued
"We tried that already"	I Felt embarrassed and humiliated
"What are you smoking"?	Made me feel Stupid
"Anyone can understand that.."	Made me feel Stupid
"That will never fly"	Made me feel Stupid
"The exec's will never go for it"	I shut down
"Get your facts straight"	I was angry
"You are missing the point..."	I felt stupid
"As I told you..."	I felt scolded
"As you know..."	I felt belittled
"No, seriously"	I felt embarrassed
"Let me play Devil's Advocate"	I got defensive

Ouch. And discounts aren't always verbal. Looking at your phone, your watch, a clock—those are discounting actions too. So is rolling your eyes; so is making eye contact with another person in the room and smiling or winking; so is flipping through (or stacking) any (unrelated) papers you have in front of you. When your associates respond to verbal or behavioral discounts with silence, they are usually doing so in an effort to self-protect from further harm. And if the norm at work is a leader-influenced discounting environment, and it isn't already detrimental to individual and collective (group) performance, it will be. Self-esteem, contingent upon positive work results, may suffer in a high-discount environment. Self-esteem degradation is often associated with depression, aggression,[15] and other behavioral problems.

Strengthening rather than discounting is important in any communication, but it's crucial when there are multiple ideas and

---

15   Crocker & Wolfe, 2001

viewpoints flowing. After all, you can't discuss problems forever, and you can't implement all the ideas you're hearing. But you can track the ideas, keep them flowing, and then narrow the options while building up (rather than tearing down) any additional input from group members. What does strengthening look like? The diagram (3.2) below shows what "strengthening" and "discounting" might look like in the context of generating ideas.

Diagram 3.2: Strengthening vs. Discounting in the Context of Idea Generation

Idea Generation
Strengthen vs. Discount

Option 1: *Strengthen* an Idea

- *I like this part of the idea*
- *How will we...?*
- *What will you do to...?*
- *How does this comply with...?*

Option 2: *Discount* an Idea
"Devil's Advocate"

- *This will never fly...*
- *We already tried this.*
- *What are you smoking?...*
- *Are you serious?...*

Let's play out the discounting approach. Say, after hearing an idea, you reply, "I heard your idea, and let me play Devil's Advocate..."

The *intent* of playing Devil's Advocate is surely to construct the best possible idea. But the Devil's Advocate tactic, while positively intended, can produce unintended negative consequences. What follows the statement, "Let me play Devil's Advocate," are generally comments or questions that point out every flaw in the presenting idea until the meeting is over and the person presenting the idea walks out of your office, head down either in shame or hiding a simmering anger.

This emotional reaction is more likely if the relationship between you and the other person is not characterized by high trust. Essentially, the Devil's Advocate process says, "Let's tear down this idea, and reduce it to the lowest denominator. You can then fix the flaws and come back so that we can start this fun all over again."

Have you really uncovered all the flaws and crafted the best possible solution? Or have you taken a mallet to a culture of voice? What was intended to be a logical process has probably become an emotional one because the Devil's Advocate interaction can threaten the associate. The emotional reaction then has physiological consequences that can interrupt the ability to focus on the task at hand—coming up with the best possible solution. What's more, others in the room, fearful of being the center of attention in a similar, demeaning way, may withhold their own ideas, or even their own criticisms of the idea on the floor, for fear that they will be treated the same way.

Now consider what might happen with a strengthening/buildup approach. Consider the idea that's been floated as the starting point. Ask yourself, "What part of this idea might work?"

When you have answered that question, state it. For example, you could say, "What I like about this idea is…" Next, if you have concerns about the idea, list them in question form. "How would we get this done within our time constraint?" "How would we finance this project?" "How many people would we need on this project to pull it off?" An inquiry process like this stimulates thinking and engages everyone in the room to help reach the best possible solution. There are two major positive consequences to this approach. First, the employee's self-esteem remains intact. Second, you're fostering a collaborative problem-solving process; everyone can contribute to the process, and no one ends up as a victim of the process.

Discounting is what we call a "shadow practice." That is, it has the opposite effect of the positive influence practices we've been advocating. Instead of encouraging and facilitating voice, it muffles, cloaks, or "shadows" it. It may be a habit (yours, your supervisor's, your organization's), but if so, it's a habit that can be broken and replaced with the much more desirable one, strengthening.

PRACTICE #6: COACH VERSUS PUNISH

A woman advancing quickly in her career at a large investment firm (so quickly that she was not aware of the glass ceiling) shared this story with us. Several years earlier, she had made a mistake that cost the firm more than four million dollars. In the immediate aftermath, she completely lost her self-esteem, and her self-image was pretty poor.

But then her manager, Bill, reviewed the account with her, and asked her for strategies to put in place to avoid this from happening again. He did not minimize the loss, nor did he minimize her feelings about it but focused on the solution rather than the problem. He acknowledged that the situation had been difficult and challenging and now the new challenge was to both contain the loss and to capture lessons.

He coached her through the crisis by demonstrating these four practices during their interaction.

1. He listened and responded with empathy to the identified situation.

2. He maintained and built up her self-esteem.

3. He asked questions to discover and uncover facts and future direction.

4. He simultaneously challenged and supported her.

In other words, he coached; he didn't punish. You can demonstrate these coaching practices also (in fact, in many ways, they draw on all of the practices we've outlined so far in this chapter).

When you discover or are made aware of a mistake:

*   **Listen** to the person describe the situation without judgment. Engage in the practice of "bracketing" (remember, that's putting your judgment or biases off to the side). Remember that people feel before they think. So, help the person or persons who made the

mistake identify feelings. "I imagine this situation has evoked quite a few feelings for you." "How are you feeling?" "What are you feeling?" Acknowledge their concerns. "Tricia, I hear and understand this has got to feel like a major setback."

- **Maintain and build employees' self-esteem** by expressing confidence. "Tricia, I know this has been a blow to you. I also know that you have successfully tackled difficulties before with optimism and skill." Provide specifics if you can, and assist with idea generation, building-up ideas that the other person shares. For example, you might say, "Let's step back for a minute and consider some approaches to (this process). What do you think?"

   Acknowledge effort and progress. For example, you might say, "You have taken good first steps in recognizing the problem source and containing the fallout."

- **Ask questions;** don't tell or state the process. For example, you might say, "You will be responsible for the repositioning strategy. How do you think you will proceed?"

- **Challenge while supporting** for high motivation and performance. Recap agreements, commitments, and the tracking process. For example, you might say, "So what I hear you saying is that over the next week you will…" "I am eager to see how you notice, accept, and overcome obstacles." You might say, "What support do you need?" "What issues do you foresee encountering?"

   Communicate your support. For example, you might say, "If you need anything else to assist you, please let me know." Commit to regular follow-up communication, progress checks, and support. For example, "Let's have a bi-weekly call to check in about progress and see if I can be your sounding board or offer other support."

Reinforce your belief in employees and their ability to execute. For example, you might say, "I believe you have a firm handle on this. How confident are you feeling?"

Your employees need to know if they can rely on you for support. Don't leave this knowledge to chance—spell it out. You can create a secure environment by demonstrating (through disclosure) humility. Employees know they aren't perfect, and they probably don't expect you to be perfect either. If you have experience in the area in which they are about to embark, express it. Ask your associate, "With what aspects of the work did you feel best and with what aspects did you struggle?" This language is non-problematic and non-threatening. Disclosing your experience gives employees permission to do the same with you (upward communication).

ANY STEP FORWARD IS A GOOD STEP

Any combination of these six leadership practices will help to shape a culture of voice in your organization. However, as one of our colleagues says, "Don't try to boil the ocean." Upgrading just one practice at a time will help. In fact, taking on one practice and implementing it with purpose will pave the way for you to take on another. Each one, in turn, will become easier to do. Each one will help your employees learn how to make their best contribution to the company.

We'll close this chapter with some reflections from someone we believe exemplifies the practices that foster a culture of voice, Warren Buffet. When Christine interviewed Warren Buffet several years ago, he shared with her his view of leadership. He offered suggestions for helping people "get out of their own way, and get out of the way of their people." Warren's approach serves as a great example of the point we will continually try to drive home—*believe and know that you are responsible for your employees' engagement more than any other factor.* We are offering guidelines based on our research and experience, but it's up to you—as it should be—to personalize what you take away.

Here are some of the thoughts Warren shared with Christine:

1. **Try to be optimistic**, *unless it is death, cruelty, or family tragedy. Otherwise, look forward to the possibilities that arise from each event.*

2. **Know that you cannot change others, but you can change yourself.** *Some people are programmed to either be very positive and jump at every moment or to sort of hang back and let events determine what happens to them. You cannot change others. So let go of what you cannot control and focus on what you can change: yourself.*

3. **If you're pessimistic, change your attitude in a hurry because the world is not going to change for you.** (He quoted Bertrand Russell): *"Success is getting what you want, and happiness is wanting what you get." If you are sour on the world, the world will be sour on you.*

4. **Do not overanalyze things**. *Actually, so many things are quite simple.*

5. **Paint your own painting.** *Every day when I get up I get to paint my painting, and nobody tells me I have to use blue paint or red paint, and nobody tells me I have to do a landscape or a seascape. I feel like Michelangelo in the Sistine Chapel – I get to paint, and it is a painting that will never be finished, but every day I get to add a little something, and it is the excitement of seeing that painting develop over time is what I do. It has nothing to do*

with money except that it has to earn decent returns over time to be a successful painting. But it is great fun not knowing exactly what I am going to paint every day.

Today, "paint your own painting" for your team to see, to help them get energized.

We have provided you with six leadership practices to help you craft your own painting, practices you can engage in each day: See it, believe it, and act upon it – paint a culture of voice and engagement. Among the results: innovation, enhanced problem-solving, knowledge transfer, and bottom-line competitive advantage. The next chapter focuses on your leadership influence. There are pragmatic tools to help you gauge the impact you have on others.

CHAPTER FOUR
ANALYZE YOUR INFLUENCE

At this point, you're ready to get into the weeds on the topic of your ability to influence others by design. To that end, this chapter offers:

-A brief story to stimulate your thinking and help you to look at your behavior dispassionately, as a third-party observer.

-A range of exercises, prompts, and other tools mapped to the leadership practices we described in the previous chapter. These will help you better understand your natural style and tendencies. In addition, we hope that they help you to encourage voice.

THE STORY

Here's the story (real, but with names held back to protect privacy). Put yourself in the shoes of the employees, the manager, and the role of outside observer. Given what you now know about cultures of voice and silence, what do you think is going on here?

What was happening? Whatever it was, it wasn't good. The employees felt this. Yet there was no communication from above. The managers in the Training Department were still actively booking sites for corporate training. They were signing contracts with vendors. They were conducting Train-the Trainer workshops. It all seemed normal, yet they sensed that something was not right.

Then came the week before the rollout of their largest International Advanced Leadership Workshop. Attendees were coming from most of the companies' locations around the world. The hotel and conference rooms had been booked. The feeling that something was wrong persisted, yet no one had asked any questions. They didn't want to know what their guts were telling them they already knew. Then came an announcement, mid-morning, from the company's leaders: "Cancel all training...all training." It had taken months to set up the calendar, enrollment processes, and arrange the venues. It took just under four hours to cancel it all. Managers felt deceived, deluded, and duped.

No one was laid off for three months, but they knew that was coming too. In an interview with us after the layoffs, one of the former managers said, "If they had just shared the situation, we could have prepared the people who were supposed to attend these programs and ourselves. We could have offered significant ideas for cutting training costs and possibly even cutting costs elsewhere. And we would have been motivated because we would have been part of the problem resolution rather than a tangential non-entity. Now they have people who aren't properly trained representing the business. How is that going to help the situation?"

Thoreau said, "Wisdom is equal to amount of reflection time." We urge you to fill in the details of this brief case study in your mind or even on paper. What might have been done differently? What ought to be done now? What specific behaviors made the most difference (positive or negative)? What could the people involved have done differently? Was there positive influence by design on the part of the leaders?

What's around the corner for this company? It is easy to evaluate when it is dispassionately written on paper. What about you? What is around the corner for YOUR company? What is the impact of YOUR influence? Wisdom equals reflection, and, we would add, action. Next, let's analyze your influence using the action tools offered in the next section.

EXERCISES, PROMPTS, AND OTHER TOOLS

The following Diagram (4.0) shows the six leadership tools to help you *Analyze Your Influence*. The diagram is circular because analyzing your influence is not a linear process. It doesn't start and end at a particular place. Each one relates to the other but none are mutually exclusive.

Diagram 4.0: Analyze Your Influence

The Table below (4.1) shows the six leadership practices we explored in the last chapter and the corresponding exercises, prompts, and tools we offer here. The rest of this chapter explains each in turn. We strongly encourage you to complete each of these exercises as thoughtfully as possible.

Table 4.1: Leadership Practices and High-Influence Tools and Exercises

Leadership Practices	High Influence Leadership Exercise
1. Maximize Your Emotional Intelligence	EI Traits
2. Strengthen Resilience	The Trust Checklist
3. Learn More than You Affirm	The Communication Investigation
4. Ask More than you Tell	Listening Assessments
5. Strengthen versus Discount	Communication Expectations Checklist
6. Coach versus Punish	The Flow Test, The Engagement Checklist, and Aristotle

1. EI TRAITS AND CONSEQUENCES
(LINKED TO MAXIMIZING YOUR EMOTIONAL INTELLIGENCE)

As we were writing this chapter, we got a call from a colleague, a Vice President in a large public company, who shared with us that he would no longer attempt to communicate honestly with his CEO. As with our other interviewees, we asked him: "What could your leader do to convince you that he has your motivation in mind?" His answer almost exactly mirrored the traits listed below (Exhibit 4.2). According to our research, employees were more apt to be motivated by leaders who were perceived to exhibit the following (or some combination of the majority of the following) 16 traits. Before you ponder these, think of a leader who influenced you in a positive way. What behaviors did he/she demonstrate that affected your engagement level?

Exhibit 4.2: EI Traits

EI Traits

❑ Humble

❑ Honest

❑ Passionate

❑ Willing to jump in themselves

❑ Sharer of initiatives

❑ Able to communicate inspirationally

❑ Loyal to team members thereby creating loyalty

❑ Confident

❑ Intelligent

❑ Possessing a high level of interpersonal skills

❑ Able to see, share and articulate the big picture

❑ Provided tools to strategically implement the big picture

❑ Gracious

❑ Courageous

❑ Modeled staying power

❑ Realized the power of "small" behaviors – as in compliments, eye contact, use of name, acknowledgement of efforts

---

With the exception of cognitive intelligence (IQ), all of the traits above are directly related to your level of Emotional Intelligence. Our research suggests that when the leadership traits above are demonstrated consistently, the leader can expect the following employee responses:

- Positive responsiveness to change increases
- Discretionary effort expands
- Knowledge transfer increases

On the flip side, our research shows that the leadership traits below (when demonstrated) were "most troubling" to employees:

- Lack of communication
- Aloofness
- Rudeness
- Failing to connect
- Discounting (putting others down)

To turn the lens on yourself, think about the most recent encounters you've had with co-workers or direct reports. Find a positive example, and look for a negative one as well. Write out what happened, what the consequences were, and why you think the situation unfolded as it did. (In other words, make yourself the star of a positive case study and a negative one.) What did you do that worked well? What could you have done differently in the negative situation? The demonstration of your Emotional Intelligence will encourage voice rather than elicit silence.

2. THE TRUST CHECKLIST
(LINKED TO STRENGTHEN RESILIENCE)

When associates feel safe because they trust you, their resilience increases, allowing them to engage and contribute during normal times and also when they're under stress. Trust is a vital ingredient in effective leadership and is linked to communication (Bass, 1985), knowledge transfer (Argote, et al., 2003), teamwork, and cooperation (Williams, 2007). Research shows that trust is the interaction among people's values, attitudes, and emotions (Jones & George, 1998). Generally, trust is characterized by the confidence one has when interacting with another person or party, such that no personal harm will occur (Bateman & Crant, 1993, Zucker, 1987).

Leaders play a pivotal role in the establishment and sustenance of trust among team members. Transformational leaders build trust with their employees. When a leader is not trusted, employees become more concerned with protecting themselves than improving their performance[16]. When team members trust their leader, they can rely on the decisions made and direction set by the leader without the distraction of protecting themselves or others from harm. When team members trust their leader, they more easily accept the goals and vision of that leader (Bennis & Nanus, 1985).

---

16   (2008) Bachman & Zaheer

From this list of Trust Enhancers below (Exhibit 4.3), pick your two strengths, the practices that you feel are demonstrated best, and the two with which you struggle most as a leader. You might be thinking, "I don't really struggle with any of these," but everyone struggles with some behavioral aspects of their work.

Exhibit 4.3: Trust Enhancers

Trust Enhancers

- ❏ Followed through on your word
- ❏ Demonstrated respect for others
- ❏ Stood up for your team
- ❏ Sought to understand by soliciting more information
- ❏ Listened to others
- ❏ Held a set of values common with the team
- ❏ Communicated your values
- ❏ Asked questions
- ❏ Gave recognition
- ❏ Removed distractions
- ❏ Shared information in a timely manner
- ❏ Involved others in the search for solutions
- ❏ Demonstrated consistency in your actions
- ❏ Chose words appropriately, no sarcasm, gossip or putdowns
- ❏ Sought simplicity – purposefully made reasoning clear
- ❏ Solicited feedback
- ❏ Appealed to others need for significance
- ❏ Was charismatic and confident
- ❏ Showed appropriate compassion
- ❏ Shared your passion
- ❏ Provided for self-governance – acknowledged your team's basic need for autonomy

Most managers with whom we work want to focus exclusively on their improvements. We think this is a mistake. We recommend that you reflect on your strength practices as well as your improvement practices. For that reason, we provide two areas below for you to identify 2-3 very specific actions you can try and results you can track for each set of practices—those that you believe are strengths and those with which you struggle.

TRY IT

Strengths: Write 2-3 commitments to action that will broaden and solidify these practices.

TRACK IT:
1. What specifically did you do differently?
2. What was the result?
3. What did you learn about yourself?

TRY IT

Upgrades: *Write 2-3 commitments to action that will reduce or eliminate your struggle practice(s). For example: If your struggle practice is "Using Sarcasm," then try reducing the number of times you use sarcasm by 50% in group meetings within the next 2 weeks.*

TRACK IT:
1. *What specifically did you do differently?*
2. *What was the result?*
3. *What did you learn about yourself?*

For example: Track the actual number of times you use sarcasm in group settings within two weeks. What did you do differently? What was the result of this change? What did you learn from it about yourself?

If you get in the habit of trying small, micro changes and tracking the results, you are less likely to feel overwhelmed by a large looming and general upgrade goal such as, "I will become a better communicator."

3. THE COMMUNICATION INVESTIGATION
(LINKED TO LEARN MORE THAN YOU AFFIRM)

"Two months ago, our CEO requested from us, the Strategic Planning Team, a partnership proposal. We were told it was urgent. We believed him and devoted all of our resources and energy to creating this. Six days ago, I submitted the proposal to our CEO, the proposal that was deemed critical by him. No feedback, absolutely no communication! None. I am more than angry, as is my team. Did I tell you it has been six days? We have spent seven weeks preparing this; we even brought in two outside consultants to coach us on alignment strategy. This has been our life. Only once did the CEO come "down" to meet with us and that was just to make sure we were aware of how important it was that we get this done. He sent one of his VP's down every day to 'check-in,' that is, to monitor us. (That did not go over too well—no trust at all.) Never any acknowledgement of our efforts, and my team sacrificed heavily. This experience was the last straw for me. I felt like a carrot had been dangled in front of us yet again. My interpretation is that our work result had little value. If that's true, I would certainly like to know why so I can learn and get better. My conclusion is that this was an exercise in futility, a lot of work for nothing. I need to be in an organization that values my work, a place where I feel significant. Based on the lack of communication, I concluded that my work had little significance here, and it was time to exit the company."

"I have contacted a search firm, and I imagine several others have too. This treatment goes against the grain of value of respect. They needed to communicate and provide some feedback, even if it was bad. Apparently, the CEO doesn't understand this need. If he had just dropped in a few times to say he appreciated what we were doing, if he had responded to our efforts to communicate, to give us little kudos or even negative feedback – some type of basic communication…."

This leader and his two direct reports exited the organization.

Communication is, by definition, a two-way street. Your communication behaviors directly impact your success as a leader and the motivation of individuals within your sphere of influence. The goal is to create a culture of trust, openness, and the application of ethical standards of excellence. Through the process of communication, voice is engaged, and your organization is positioned to prepare for any curve ball it is thrown.

Below (Exhibit 4.4) are 11 vital and difficult questions which will require self-reflection. Ask yourself, then, ask your team:

Exhibit 4.4: Communication Self-Reflection Questions

1. Has your organization ever paid the price for ineffective communication? If yes, what was the price (consequence)?
2. Pick a recent meeting, or conversation you had with your associates or direct reports. Can you demonstrate your understanding of the message you received, both fact and feeling?
3. How do you know if someone has listened to you?
4. What are your own barriers to good communication?
5. What does your organization do to encourage communication? What does it fail to do?
6. How do you know when you have clear communication?
7. How do you teach them how to ask for what they need/want?
8. When did you last interpret others non-verbal signals? Are certain colleagues "easier to read" than others? Why is that?
9. How do you distinguish between intentions and behaviors?
10. How do you get others to share information and ideas? When was the last time you did this, and what happened?
11. How do you tell when your employees or colleagues are: defensive, just present, attentive, or engaged?

As you ponder the implications of your responses, consider past difficult times with your employees. Consider problems you have incurred with projects, client engagements, or team initiatives. According to our research, the root cause analysis of the majority of these difficulties relates to ineffective communication.

Below, we describe four levels of communication. Existing research supported by our interview and coaching data suggests that understanding these levels will help you to better interpret how your approach to communication affects others (Brady, Steeples & Fleming, 2005). The four levels are determined by your unconscious and conscious choices of purpose. That is, they incorporate *intra*personal communication (your internal dialogue, which cues you to select a level of communication) and *inter*personal communication (what you intentionally offer others). Your internal dialogue is shaped by your self-esteem, by past experiences, by current perceived realities, and by your environment. Becoming conscious of your internal dialogue can help you develop more open and effective interpersonal communication.

LEVELS OF COMMUNICATION

Level 1. Superficial. This constitutes polite, idle chat. This is when you communicate about the weather, sports, and other safe topics. This is advantageous with new acquaintances or if you want to play it completely safe. It does serve a purpose and can be a contributor to social capital.

Level 2. Information-based. This involves the sharing of facts. Information and facts are important if the right ones are truly uncovered at the information share level. However, if communication stops here, opportunities for voice decrease. In order for associates to be truly engaged, they need to know they can voice their ideas, concerns, and opinions. Therefore, we need to move to Levels 3 and 4.

Communication at levels 3 and 4 requires a leap across a chasm of trust and engagement.

Level 3. Thought-based. This is when people make a true effort to engage with one another. They open up and share ideas, opinions, and perspectives. If a culture of voice is present, this communication will not be perceived as a risk but rather valid and necessary for the organization's higher purpose. If people are rebuffed here, they will immediately go back to a superficial or fact level, which often is a symptom of a culture of silence.

Level 4. Value-based—Emotional. At this level, people share their feelings about a problem or opportunity often based on values. This level is not about *being* emotional. Rather, it is about sharing emotions and the gut instincts that give us insight. It is a "foundation" level for the building of relationships, for a culture of voice. It takes trust for people to share their values, worries, new ideas, problems, needs, their hopes, and their dreams related to their "job."

Truly effective communication incorporates level 2 but takes place at level 3 and level 4. Leaders who encourage an appropriate part of their communication to take place at these levels can attain and sustain high performance. The curiosity fostered by a culture of voice encourages high levels of interaction and involvement versus isolation and speculation that can arise when there is a lack of communication. Leaders who use these levels of communication tap into that which cannot be readily seen—the uniqueness, imagination, and commitment of their employees.

Consider these examples:

Level 1. Superficial.

"Hi. Great weather today. How was your commute?"

Level 2. Information.

"There are fifty expense reports waiting to be processed."

Level 3. Thought.

"I think that there is something wrong with our accounts payable system."

Now at least, and at last, someone is opening up, revealing something about themselves in terms of their ability to reason and speculate. This level of vulnerability deserves honor and respect.

Level 4. Value-based—Emotional.

"It does not feel right to take on another project. Something is not right about this, but I cannot get a handle on it."

A statement like this requires trust between the employee and the leader. When it exists, the leader can help uncover the reason(s) for discomfort (in this case) by probing with open-ended questions to uncover the root cause (information) of the underlying issue.

4. LISTENING ASSESSMENTS
(LINKED TO ASK MORE THAN YOU TELL)

"One friend, one person who is truly understanding, who takes the trouble to listen to us as we consider our problems, can change our whole outlook on the work."

Dr. Elton Mayo of the Mayo Clinic

Too many people feel that they have never been listened to. Imagine the power you have as a leader to create engagement and encourage voice if you are an effective listener.

How well do you listen? To answer this question, complete the following self-assessment diagnostics below (Exhibits 4.5 & 4.6). To learn more, have a few trusted advisors or colleagues complete these assessments of your listening behaviors as well.

Exhibit 4.5: Listening Assessment #1

Listening Assessment #1

When listening to someone else, do I:	Yes	No
1. Daydream?	❑	❑
2. Forget most of the information I hear within 24 hours?	❑	❑
3. Tune out if the information is too difficult or perceived to be irrelevant?	❑	❑
4. Get distracted easily?	❑	❑
5. Judge the speaker?	❑	❑
6. React too quickly?	❑	❑
7. Get impatient?	❑	❑
8. Finish the statements of others who speak slowly?	❑	❑
9. Interrupt?	❑	❑
10. Let my emotions preoccupy me?	❑	❑
11. Let the speaker's mannerisms annoy me?	❑	❑
12. Think about what I am going to say next?	❑	❑
Total:	___	___

The more "yes" answers you have, the more the red flag rises. Even one "yes" can indicate that you are not listening effectively (Johnson & Bechler, 1998). To get more out of this assessment, ask yourself if any "yes" behaviors occur when you are listening to a particular individual or when you are in a particular type of meeting or context.

For example, when people try to quit smoking, they are often advised to change their daily routines, even a little bit, to get them out of the habit of cueing themselves that it's time to light up. For example, if they have their first cigarette of the day when they're brewing morning coffee, they're told to try going out for coffee instead, or even moving the coffee-maker to the other side of the room. Anything to help them become more aware of the context, and the cue, so they can spot it and counter it.

If you usually stay behind your desk when an employee enters your office needing your attention, try moving, even a little bit, to increase your attention to them and decrease your distractions (PC monitor, telephone, mobile device).

Exhibit 4.6: Listening Assessment #2

Listening Assessment #2		
When listening to someone else, do I:	**Yes**	**No**
1. Make a commitment to listen?	❏	❏
2. Maintain good eye contact with the speaker?	❏	❏
3. Understand the speaker's behavioral/ communication style?	❏	❏
4. Respect differences in the speaker's appearance, word choice and style from my own?	❏	❏
5. Accept responsibility for the communication process?	❏	❏
6. Have a process for capturing their information, (take notes on a white board, a pad, the computer)?	❏	❏
7. Read the speaker's body language?	❏	❏
8. Ask questions?	❏	❏
9. Listen for the speaker's intention?	❏	❏
10. Check for accuracy of interpretation?	❏	❏
Total:	___	___

In this list, unlike the previous one, a "yes" response is positive. Again, consider how your answers may change if you are talking with different people in different contexts. Specifically, what can you do differently to turn even one "No" into a "Yes?"

5. COMMUNICATION EXPECTATIONS CHECKLIST
(LINKED TO STRENGTHEN VERSUS DISCOUNT)

The following checklist (Exhibit 4.7), based on our research, highlights what people expect from great communicators.

Exhibit 4.7: Communication Expectations Checklist

Communication Expectations Checklist

❏ Acknowledgement of audience needs
(Why are they there, and how will they use what they learn?)

❏ A look at the big picture

❏ A well-thought out statement of purpose

❏ A well-organized, concise delivery

❏ Examples of supporting evidence

❏ Difficult questions met head on

❏ A firm close, focused on theme and action

❏ Natural and respectful delivery

❏ Confidence and conviction

Pick two items that you want to work on first and know why. Remember, be specific about what you Try and how to Track your progress, and don't try to boil the ocean.

6. THE FLOW TEST, THE ENGAGEMENT CHECKLIST, AND ARISTOTLE
(LINKED TO COACH VERSUS PUNISH)

"Most US companies are over-managed and under-led."

John P. Kotter, 1998, Harvard Business Review

We agreed with Professor Kotter, and we still believe this sentiment to be true. Many leaders give in to ordinary versus exceptional because they cannot visualize what exceptional would be. Managers are transactional: they do things the "right way." They deal with functions to ensure stability and order. Leaders are transformational: they determine the right things to do because they can visualize what's over the horizon, changes, problems, and opportunities that need to be discussed.

To get a better sense of whether (and to what extent) you make deliberate connections between the big picture and the day-to-day, complete the Flow Test below:

THE FLOW TEST

Flow = engagement. Flow is doing what you love, what you are good at, knowing that there is a current and future need for it and an appreciation for it and you. Psychologist Mihaly Csikszentmihalyi, who coined the term in this context, says it is the "Optimal Experience." (M. Csikszentmihalyi, 1990). When you are in a state of flow, you basically are unstoppable. Your energy, enthusiasm, and focus define you in the moment.

Here are the qualities we have come to identify in people who are in a state of Flow:

1. Autonomous. They believe that they have control over most of the major decisions within their sphere of influence. They are the masters of their fate.

2. Authentic. They know that they can be themselves. They do not act based on the opinion of others, but rather they are true to themselves through conscious applied reasoning.

3. Focused. They do not get sidelined. They keep their eye on the goal.

4. Aligned. Their actions reflect their values.

5. Integrated. They fulfill their personal as well as professional needs to create a balanced life.

6. Discerning. They know that the pursuit of excellence is a matter of clear choice.

7. Grateful. They can identify positive aspects of the organization.

8. Celebratory. They know and embrace the idea that celebrations are part of a culture of voice.

In other words, they are engaged.

Answer the following Flow Test questions regarding your job:

- · What are you good at (Collins, 2001)?
- · What do you have a passion for (Collins, 2001)?
- · What gives you intrinsic return?
- · What gives you an extrinsic return?
- · Is there a current need for your job?
- · Will there be a need in the future for your job?

If you have a uniform "yes" response to all six of these questions, chances are you are fully engaged. How would your employees respond to the Flow Test? If they respond "No" to any of these questions, they may not be fully engaged.

THE ENGAGEMENT CHECKLIST

Remember a time when you went into a meeting without much enthusiasm. Did you ever leave that type of a meeting engaged? If so, we'd bet that your "conversion" was due in large part to the communication skills and relationship-building personality of the leader. (Yes, sure, it might have been the quality of the coffee, too, but really, it was more about the ability of the meeting's leader to coach and persuade rather than dictate and drone.) Think of a leader who has inspired you in a positive way. How did they do that? What behaviors did they exhibit?

We asked managers who participated in our High-Influence Leadership® Programs (globally) to name the practices demonstrated by those leaders who had the greatest (positive) impact on their engagement level. Fourteen behaviors emerged as the most often mentioned among the 750 managers we interviewed, and they are listed below (Exhibit 4.8). As you read through this list, identify the two practices your exemplary leader did most? Least? Then, select the two practices that you (believe) you do most and least. Lastly, identify the two with which you struggle most .

Exhibit 4.8: The Engagement Checklist

The Engagement Check List

❑ Believed in me and demonstrated that belief

❑ Had my best interests in mind

❑ Clearly explained what was expected

❑ Trusted me

❑ Articulated a focused and compelling vision

❑ Listened to my suggestions

❑ Honored their commitment

❑ Asked for my input

❑ Shared similar past experiences

❑ Acknowledged me

❑ Looked outside the box

❑ Challenged me

❑ Stood up for their beliefs

❑ Shared reality both the positive and negative aspects

ARISTOTLE

We'll close this chapter with some thoughts from the Greek philosopher Aristotle. According to Aristotle, there are three appeals, or modes of persuasion: ethos, pathos, and logos.

Ethos: an appeal to ethics. You are credible, and you have a good reason to do what you are setting out to do.

Pathos: an appeal to emotion. You connect with your team.

Logos: an appeal to the use of reason. Your communication is logical.

When you are communicating to influence, it's important to incorporate all three:

Ethos: "Our collective fifty-five years of research, application, and experience make us more than qualified to write on the topic of silence. We feel it is important to share what we have learned, in the hope that it will be useful to others."

Pathos: "Your power to break corporate silence will be the key to your ability to break through to excellence versus simply surviving. Think what we can do for our customers/clients if we excel versus just getting our jobs done. Your contribution is valuable."

Logos: "Our research methods have been peer-reviewed, and findings are trustworthy and reliable. People are motivated by: meaningful work, autonomy, a sense of belonging, recognition, and the safety to have a voice in important work-related issues."

Use the High-Influence tools and exercises from this chapter to regularly "Analyze Your Influence." Chapter Five provides self-reflection diagnostics to sustain a culture of voice in your organization.

CHAPTER FIVE
SELF-REFLECTION, INSIGHT, AND IMPACT

"The unexamined life isn't worth living"
- Socrates

Based on your work done in the first four chapters, you are now positioned to make the changes needed to sustain a culture of voice. Sustaining this culture in your organization is actually more about you than it is about your employees or colleagues in the C-Suite. This chapter focuses on enhancing the ability to constantly reflect on your behaviors and gain increased insight into the effect you may have on others. Specifically, the Personal Change Model® will enable you to tie together all of the self-reflections, assessments, results, and tools from previous chapters to make significant personal change.

Does that sound as if we're asking you to be self-centered? Well, we are, but for a very good reason. "Do as I say, not as I do," doesn't work when you're trying to establish a healthy organizational climate and behavioral norms for a business unit or an entire organization. If you're leading a company, a department, or a work unit, the ability to self-reflect and gain insights increases the chances of making positive behavior changes that can create and sustain a culture of voice. We begin with two types of self-reflection.

TWO TYPES OF SELF-REFLECTION: IM AND AM

Ideally, self-reflection happens both In-the-Moment (IM)—in real time as any given situation is unfolding—and also After-the-Moment (AM)—after an interaction has occurred. Developing your ability to self-reflect in both contexts can increase your chances of self-correcting behavior that, left unchecked, might have had regrettable results. You'll also improve your hindsight. Despite the old saying, hindsight is only 20/20 if you have a clear view!

Then, if you have inadvertently taken a step in the wrong direction and recognize it, you will have a choice of either (a) owning and resolving the damage done, and/or (b) making a commitment to do it better next time. Let us be clear: "a" is the correct answer, and "b" is just a nice bonus that doesn't carry weight until "next time" comes to pass. This quote from Henry Wadsworth Longfellow explains why:

> "We judge ourselves by our intentions;
> Others judge us by our behaviors.
> We don't see our behaviors;
> Others don't see our intentions."

We think this passage captures the root of misunderstandings that can cause relationship breakdowns if left unresolved. Keeping In-the-Moment (IM) self-reflection in mind, consider these five questions about your leadership influence:

IN-THE-MOMENT

1. Is my tone (volume and intensity) encouraging or discouraging participation in this conversation?

2. What is the observable body language of others (i.e. leaning in or pushing away)?

3. Is their body language a response to my behavior?

4. At what level (high, medium, low) am I listening to others' views and opinions?

5. Am I "telling" more than I am "asking"? If yes, is that behavior appropriate?

A self-reflective leader will be asking and answering these questions in the back of his or her mind as any interaction unfolds. He or she will also be course-correcting—based on that background dialogue—to try to make sure that he or she is encouraging a culture of voice.

Now, keeping After-the-Moment (AM) self-reflection in mind, consider these five questions about your leadership influence:

AFTER-THE-MOMENT

1. Was my tone encouraging or discouraging participation during the conversation?

    a. What did I notice that might have indicated an encouraging tone or discouraging tone?

    b. Did I see any "bovine stares?"

2. What was the observable body language of others in general?

3. Was the body language of others a response to my behavior?

4. How much did I listen relative to talking?

5. If I "Told" more than I "Asked," why was that approach appropriate?

As the leader, you will be in a position to take ownership of any behaviors that may have had an undesirable effect on others or on the process in which you were engaged. Hoping everyone will forget is wishful thinking—they won't. The employee culture remembers everything you do and say. It tells stories about everything you do and say. Taking ownership means resolving any unintended consequences. The good news is that in most cases, you will be able to do so.

What does that conversation sound like? It starts by addressing the party who was (or parties who were) affected most by sharing your self-reflections and clarifying your intentions. For instance:

"Yesterday in our staff meeting, I realize that when John said he thought we should start tracking outstanding IT issues, I interrupted and said, 'Not going to happen.' I noticed that everyone was quiet after that. My intention was NOT to shut

everyone down. I realize now that my quick reaction without hearing John out and listening to his idea had a bad effect. My intention is to hear everyone and to learn from you and encourage your input – not shut it down."

Chances are you have probably engaged in some form of self-reflection. But unstructured self-reflection can lead to unproductive and repetitive rumination about thoughts, feelings, and behaviors. To understand in more depth the kind of purposeful self-reflection that leads to useful insight, take the Self-Assessment and Insights Survey (SRIS) in Appendix A. The SRIS shows the level of need and desire to engage in the self-reflection process and the extent to which you gain insights from self-reflection.

It's also important to try to get some direct feedback from your colleagues and direct reports (or customers, or other people with whom you interact on a regular basis at work). Some leaders are fortunate enough to be able to participate in formal development programs, complete with coaches, third-party interviews, surveys, and other techniques that elicit such feedback. But those formal supports aren't available to everyone; some companies simply lack the resources. In their absence (depending on the type of culture you're working in), self-reflection must rely in large part on you being able to interpret others' tacit feedback—body language, willingness to speak up (or not), and so forth—at least until you are able to establish enough of a culture of voice to support reliable internal feedback channels.

High-Influence Leaders demonstrate self-regulation In-the-Moment and After-the-Moment. Survey scores that indicate a high level and need (desire) for self-reflection and insight may indicate higher degrees of self-regulation or self-control—a key characteristic of the High-Influence Leader. The case below illustrates a deep level of self-reflection and insights leading to personal change.

CASE STUDY: JAMES

The following brief case study shows how AM self-reflection helped one leader bridge a communication gap with his direct reports. It also introduces a simple tool that is very useful in AM reflecting: the Personal Change Model®. The Personal Change Model® helps people see (quite literally) how their beliefs and values manifest themselves in their actions.

"James," (pseudonym) is a senior leader in a technology company. Early on in his tenure, he established certain procedures for his direct reports to follow, including providing him with weekly updates on all outstanding and critical projects.

James was fortunate enough to have third-party assistance, and through those channels, he learned that his direct reports experienced his reporting requirements as micromanaging. They felt as though they were being constantly watched and were resentful. They also worried that they spent so much time on the reports that they weren't able to concentrate fully on what they considered to be value-added work.

James was stunned when he heard this news. But it wasn't until he began to engage in AM reflection, however, that he was able to look back purposefully and objectively on his actions and their effect.

To do so, he used the Personal Change Model (Diagram 5.0). First, he filled in the beliefs, values, and actions section. Then, he took the particulars of the situation at hand and filled in the feedback section. These elements, seen together, began to help James gain a broader perspective of his impact. With the model in front of him, he was able to see how his innate beliefs that "people can't be left alone and trusted to do the right thing," and that "leaders are supposed to know what's going on all the time," coupled with his most important values (structure and order), influenced his behaviors. These beliefs and values had led him to impose those weekly status reports along with regular check-ins and other controlling practices.

He was also able to see how those beliefs and values had formed. James had a very tumultuous upbringing by two alcoholic parents. He learned at a very early age that if he didn't care for his younger siblings during his parents' drinking binges, they would be in danger. Structure became his active survival mechanism in life, and his early adolescent experiences transferred into his adult life in an organization where hundreds of people relied on his support and direction.

When James used the model—essentially performing a root cause analysis—he was able to see his employees' point of view and absorb the feedback. Armed with that insight, he was then able to talk openly with his staff and convey why he had put all of the procedures in place. Listening and using IM self-reflection during that conversation and other subsequent meetings, he was able to encourage brainstorming that led to a solution. Together, James and his team created a system that worked for them all.

Without examining the root cause of his observable behavior, any change James made in his approach would likely have been superficial, like window dressing. It might have encouraged a culture of voice for a while, helping in a few situations, but in a relatively short time period, the progress he made would have eroded. The likelihood of recidivism is very high without root cause analysis.

We would never advocate dropping all control mechanisms, but as the case of James shows, it's important to examine the reasons why you want them—or any other processes—in the first place. IM self-reflection would have helped James avoid the detrimental consequence of associate discontent and disengagement. AM reflection—with follow through—did help him after the fact.

The Personal Change Model used in this case, is illustrated (Diagram 5.0) and defined below.

Diagram 5.0: Personal Change Model

BREAKING CORPORATE SILENCE

The Personal Change Model is centered on the pyramid of beliefs, values, and actions (behaviors) defined in Chapter One. Feedback, either formal or informal, and goal-directed self-reflection and insights result in new (self) knowledge and new actions. Transformation, at the change pinnacle, is achieved when feedback, self-reflection, and insights are used to do root cause analysis of your (observable) actions, the values that drive your actions, and the beliefs that drive your values. The Personal Change Model is perpetual. The learning that is part of the personal change process should never stop. Perpetual learning requires a combination of both critical and pattern thinking.

PATTERN THINKING AND CRITICAL THINKING

Pattern thinking and critical thinking are used to complement reflective thinking. Like reflective thinking, they are based on the premise that action without reflection is thoughtless, and reflection without action is passive. Pattern and critical thinking are defined next.

Pattern Thinking

Here's a quick way to grasp pattern thinking. Look at the image below (Exhibit 5.1). What is it?

Exhibit 5.1: Pattern Thinking

Now look at this image (Exhibit 5.2). What is it?

Exhibit 5.2: Pattern Thinking

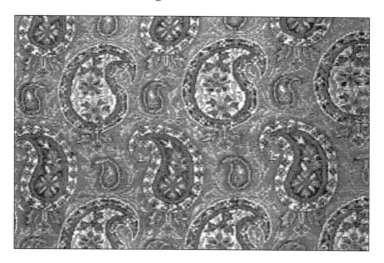

As you can see, the picture in Exhibit 5.1 is one element of the entire paisley image or pattern. The picture in Exhibit 5.2 is clearly the entire paisley pattern. Pattern thinking is the ability to step back from a single element of any given situation or problem and recognize a pattern (if there is one). For example, routines such as daily status report reviews can prevent us from seeing the bigger picture. When we are so focused on the repetitive task of reviewing report details, we may not see observable patterns until we step back and look at the same data with a broader view. Pattern thinking, when applied to individual leaders, can help you to recognize behavioral patterns that may have either desirable or undesirable effects.

CRITICAL THINKING

Critical Thinking is the process of questioning your "default" assumptions. For example, when conducting experiential learning projects in executive development workshops, one of the projects we use involves a box of puzzle pieces, which, when assembled, shows a map of the United States. We instruct the group to complete the project quickly, and we explain that everything they need to complete it successfully is contained in the materials they will receive. We announce the project start time and drop bags of puzzle pieces on tables. Invariably, the leaders begin to assemble the puzzle without asking any questions. We ask four times, "How are you doing?" We generally receive the same answer, a variation of "just fine, thanks." When they finish, we ask if they have met the objective, and they generally reply, "Yes."

"Have you met the objective?" is a trick question. How do they know that they've met the objective? They never asked about it! Their response is not necessarily bad, but it is an example of operating within one's mental model without questioning assumptions. Puzzle pieces are supposed to be "assembled." When we tell leaders that they have not met the objective, they're very surprised. They ask, "How could that be? Puzzle pieces are to be assembled—why would anyone do anything else with puzzle pieces?" It is not what we, the facilitators (the client in this case) wanted from these leaders. We had a set of success criteria that was not questioned but rather assumed based on mental models and a confirming orientation (Chapter 3) that kept the leaders from questioning their assumptions about the client's (facilitator in this case) wants and specifications.

A better question would be: What prevents so many smart leaders from questioning their assumptions when solving problems and making decisions? Critical thinking helps us challenge our mental models so that they do not block our ability to react successfully to new and different situations.

A DIFFICULT JOURNEY . . . ONE WORTH MAKING

We'll offer one more story, this one about a man named Alan, whose self-reflection efforts are paying off in spades.

Alan is a vice president of production in a global consumer products company with 2200 associates relying on his leadership and direction. We had the privilege of working with him several years ago. Alan was hired to help the business unit transition to a new hardware platform. He successfully managed a similar enterprise-wide project at his previous company. Alan was confident that his previous experience, if applied, would be effective on this current project.

Based on that experience, he had a mental model of what a successful systems implementation would look like. He also had a mental model for leadership practices that lead to successful project completion. Unfortunately, those models were flawed—based as they were on unchecked assumptions he had made about his new organization's culture.

Specifically, his current company culture was collaborative; people were used to providing input; key stakeholders were accustomed to being consulted and being a part of the decision-making process. As a result, the success of any initiative was measured both on process and outcomes. Leadership practices could be perceived as "failing" even if a project achieved the desired results in terms of performance. Alan was shocked when he received feedback from his direct reports that he was overly opinionated, forceful, and unyielding to other intelligent sources of knowledge within his organization.

Initially defensive (who wouldn't be!), Alan nonetheless realized the need to self-reflect and to gain insights about his leadership assumptions and to be open to learning a better way to improve his influence. He did so with gusto; there's really no other way to put it. After acknowledging and legitimizing his current state, we suggested a transition process that included deep introspection into his actions, values, and underlying beliefs about his worldview at work. This leader dove into the process. He was unrelenting with his self-assessment using the Personal Change Model, and he was diligent with the "Try-It-and-Track-It" development process. Shortly thereafter, he was able to make better sense of his actions and the level of influence and impact they had on his direct reports and the organization as a whole. He assessed what (leader practices) worked and specifically, which ones needed further upgrades.

When leaders are open to learning about themselves, questioning their assumptions and mental models, seeking to understand the implications of their actions on business results and employees, they have a high probability of achieving High-Influence Leadership®. When you practice and improve AM and IM reflection and insights, you should begin to notice that others are contributing more in meetings, holding back less. You should start to hear more minority views and opinions and generally see more idea sharing. If these outcomes sound beneficial to you, your team, and your business, then it's time to start the IM and AM reflection and insights practices until they become a habit.

Effective and sustained transformation involves using all parts of the Personal Change Model to conduct meaningful self-reflection, gain goal-oriented insights, and conduct root cause analysis of your observable behaviors, values, and underlying beliefs. All of this data together will help you sustain personal change.

THE CONCLUSION
YOU, THE HIGH-INFLUENCE LEADER — BUILDING CORPORATE VOICE

NOW IMAGINE.

Imagine your organization with a culture of voice: open communication, a high-trust environment, rapid information sharing, openness to feedback, fully-informed decision making, resilience, and sustained competitive advantage.

NOW IMAGINE.

Imagine yourself as a High-Influence Leader.....a leader who is fully aware of the impact of his/her behaviors in-the-moment and after-the-moment; a leader who can self-correct; a leader who makes others feel safe, respected, and significant; a leader who can self-reflect, gain insight and decide how he/she will consciously impact others and have a more profound positive influence on business results.

NOW STOP...STOP IMAGINING AND CONSIDER:

Consider your beliefs, values and behaviors.

Consider your past wake (influence). Visualize your future wake (influence).

You have the information you need to break corporate silence because now is your time, and it is your responsibility. It is your time to assume the role of a High-Influence Leader; it is your responsibility to move your organization from a climate of silence to a climate of voice—your responsibility to raise employee commitment to the highest level possible. Use your emotional intelligence, strengthen your resilience, learn more than you affirm, ask more than you tell, build more than discount, and coach more than punish. Go back to the assessments, work with the Try It and Track It® tool, and as we have said, most importantly, commit to regular reflection and insight using the Personal Change Model. Do not try to boil the ocean, but focus on one change at a time. The time is now to Break Corporate Silence.

NOW ACT.

Use the Personal Change Model® now to create your legacy—a legacy of employee voice and engagement. Take the challenge, and meet the challenge. You have the vision, you have the knowledge, and you have the tools. It is your responsibility and your obligation to break the silence. Too much is riding on this—not just for you, but for your employees, your peers, and your customers. Build a culture of voice now.

IF NOT YOU, THEN WHO? AND IF NOT NOW, THEN WHEN?

With our sincere thanks and best wishes,

Rob & Christine

APPENDIX

Please read the following questions and circle the response that indic.
Try to be accurate, but work quickl

THERE ARE NO "WRONG" OR "RIGHT" ANSWI

BE SURE TO ANSWER EVERY QUESTION FOR EACH QUESTION

1.	I don't often think about my thoughts
2.	I am not really interested in analyzing my behavior
3.	I am usually aware of my thoughts
4.	I'm often confused about the way that I really feel about things
5.	It is important for me to evaluate the things that I do
6.	I usually have a very clear idea about why I've behaved in a certain way
7.	I am very interested in examining what I think about
8.	I rarely spend time in self-reflection
9.	I'm often aware that I'm having a feeling, but I often don't quite know what i
10.	I frequently examine my feelings
11.	My behavior often puzzles me
12.	It is important to me to try to understand what my feelings mean
13.	I don't really think about why I behave in the way that I do
14.	Thinking about my thoughts makes me more confused
15.	I have a definite need to understand the way that my mind works
16.	I frequently take time to reflect on my thoughts
17.	Often I find it difficult to make sense of the way I feel about things
18.	It is important to me to be able to understand how my thoughts arise
19.	I often think about the way I feel about things
20.	I usually know why I feel the way I do

E = Engagement in self-reflection: **N** = Need

ring instructions shown)

e degree to which you agree or disagree with each of the statements.
ot spend too much time on any question

ONLY YOUR OWN PERSONAL PERSPECTIVE

ONLY CIRCLE ONE ANSWER

(R)	(E)	Disagree Strongly	1	Disagree	2	Disagree Slightly	3	Agree Slightly	4	Agree	5	Agree Strongly	6
(R)	(N)	Disagree Strongly	1	Disagree	2	Disagree Slightly	3	Agree Slightly	4	Agree	5	Agree Strongly	6
(I)		Disagree Strongly	1	Disagree	2	Disagree Slightly	3	Agree Slightly	4	Agree	5	Agree Strongly	6
(R)	(I)	Disagree Strongly	1	Disagree	2	Disagree Slightly	3	Agree Slightly	4	Agree	5	Agree Strongly	6
(N)		Disagree Strongly	1	Disagree	2	Disagree Slightly	3	Agree Slightly	4	Agree	5	Agree Strongly	6
(I)		Disagree Strongly	1	Disagree	2	Disagree Slightly	3	Agree Slightly	4	Agree	5	Agree Strongly	6
(N)		Disagree Strongly	1	Disagree	2	Disagree Slightly	3	Agree Slightly	4	Agree	5	Agree Strongly	6
(R)	(E)	Disagree Strongly	1	Disagree	2	Disagree Slightly	3	Agree Slightly	4	Agree	5	Agree Strongly	6
(R)		Disagree Strongly	1	Disagree	2	Disagree Slightly	3	Agree Slightly	4	Agree	5	Agree Strongly	6
(E)		Disagree Strongly	1	Disagree	2	Disagree Slightly	3	Agree Slightly	4	Agree	5	Agree Strongly	6
(R)	(I)	Disagree Strongly	1	Disagree	2	Disagree Slightly	3	Agree Slightly	4	Agree	5	Agree Strongly	6
(N)		Disagree Strongly	1	Disagree	2	Disagree Slightly	3	Agree Slightly	4	Agree	5	Agree Strongly	6
(R)	(E)	Disagree Strongly	1	Disagree	2	Disagree Slightly	3	Agree Slightly	4	Agree	5	Agree Strongly	6
(R)	(I)	Disagree Strongly	1	Disagree	2	Disagree Slightly	3	Agree Slightly	4	Agree	5	Agree Strongly	6
(N)		Disagree Strongly	1	Disagree	2	Disagree Slightly	3	Agree Slightly	4	Agree	5	Agree Strongly	6
(E)		Disagree Strongly	1	Disagree	2	Disagree Slightly	3	Agree Slightly	4	Agree	5	Agree Strongly	6
(R)	(I)	Disagree Strongly	1	Disagree	2	Disagree Slightly	3	Agree Slightly	4	Agree	5	Agree Strongly	6
(N)		Disagree Strongly	1	Disagree	2	Disagree Slightly	3	Agree Slightly	4	Agree	5	Agree Strongly	6
(E)		Disagree Strongly	1	Disagree	2	Disagree Slightly	3	Agree Slightly	4	Agree	5	Agree Strongly	6
(I)		Disagree Strongly	1	Disagree	2	Disagree Slightly	3	Agree Slightly	4	Agree	5	Agree Strongly	6

lf-reflection: **I** = Insight: **R** = Reverse scored

Scoring Instructions

Summed scores are used.

Step 1.

- **Reverse score those items marked (R).**
- An original score of "1" would become "6"; "2" would become "5"; "3" becomes "4" and visa versa.
- Mark the Reversed Score next to the item number.

Step 2.

- **Sum the scores for each subscale.**
- **Transfer your scores to the table below**

Engagement in Self-reflection Sub-scale – Items: **1(R)**, **8(R)**, 10, **13(R)**, 16, 19

N = Need for Self-reflection Sub-scale – Items: **2(R)**, 5, 7, 12, 15, 18

I = Insight Sub-scale – Items: 3, **4(R)** , 6, **9(R)**, 11(R), **14(R)**, **17(R)**, 20

Engagement in Self-Reflection	Need for Self-Reflection	Insight
1 (R):	2 (R):	3:
8 (R):	5:	4 (R):
10:	7:	6:
13 (R):	12:	9 (R):
16:	15:	11 (R):
19:	18:	14 (R):
		17 (R):
		20:
TOTAL:		

Score Key

Level of SR Engagement	Need for Self-Reflection	Insight
(6-15) Disengaged from SR	**(6-15)** Low SR Need	**(8-20)** Low Insight Level
(16-27) Slightly to Moderately Engaged in SR	**(16-27)** Slight to Moderate SR Need	**(21-36)** Moderate Insight Level
(28-36) Highly Engaged in SR	**(28-36)** High SR Need	**(37-48)** High Insight Level

SELF-REFLECTION AND INSIGHTS SCALE
SCORE KEY: RESULTS INTERPRETATION

Level of SR Engagement

A score between 6-15 indicates that you most likely have a low level of engagement in the self-reflection process. Self-reflection is known to be an important component of the self-regulatory process. A low level of self-reflection engagement can make it difficult to change behaviors that could be counterproductive and or contribute to a culture of silence.

A score between 16-27 indicates that you have a moderate tendency for self-focused self-reflection vs. problem-focused self-reflection. At this level you are focused more on your behaviors than on the learning (insights) and ways to fix behavioral problems.

A score between 28-36 indicates that you regularly and quite naturally (automatically) engage in both self-focused and problem-focused self-reflection process.

Need for Self-Reflection

A score between 6-15 indicates a low need for the self-focused or problem-focused self-reflection.

A score between 16-27 indicates a moderate need for self-focused and problem-focused self-reflection.

A score between 28-36 indicates a high need for self-focused and problem-focused self-reflection.

Insight

A score between 8-20 indicates a low level of insight. Insight involves self-evaluation that can then lead to personal (behavior) change.

A score between 21-36 indicates a moderate level of insight after self-reflection. Insights involve self-evaluation that can then lead to personal (behavior) change.

A score between 37-48 indicates a high level (automatic) of insight as part of the self-reflection process. Insights involve self-evaluation that can then lead to (behavior) change.

REFERENCE LIST

Argote, L., McEvily, B., & Reagans, R. (2003). Managing Knowledge in Organizations: An Integrative Framework and Review of Emerging Themes. Management Science, 49(4), 571-582.

Axelrod, R. (1994). The evolution of cooperation. New York: Basic Books.

Bass, B.M. (1985). Leadership and performance beyond expectations. New York: Free Press.

Bateman, T.S. & Crant, J. M. (1993). The proactive component of organizational behavior: A measure and correlates. Journal of Organizational Behavior, 14: 103-118.

Bennis, W., & Nanus, B. (1985). Leaders: The strategy for taking charge. New York: Harper & Row.

Brady, N.C., Steeples, T. & Fleming, K. (2005), Effects of pluralistic communication levels on initiation and repair of communication in children with disabilities. Journal of Speech, Hearing and Language Research, 48, 1098-1113.

Burris, E. R., Deter, J. R. & Chiaburu, D. S. (2008). Quitting before leaving: The mediating effects of psychological attachment and detachment on voice. Journal of Applied Psychology, 93(4), 912-922.

Collins, J. (2001). Good to Great. New York: Harper Collins.

Gosling, J. & Mintzberg, H. (2006). Management education as if both matter. Management Learning, 37(4), 419-228.

Csikszentmihalyi, M. (1990). Flow - The psychology of optimal experience. New York: Harper Perennial).

Crocker , J. & Major, B. (1989). Social stigma and self-esteem: The self-protective properties of stigma. Psychological Review, 96(4), 608-630.

Crocker, J. & Wolf, C. T. (2001). Contingencies of self-worth. Psychological Review, 108(3), 593-623.

Cropanzano, R., Bowen, D. E. & Gilliland, S. W. (2007). The management of organizational justice. Academy of Management Perspectives, 21(4), 34-48.

Husserl, E. (1931). Ideas. (W. R. Boyce Gobson, Trans.). London: George Allen & Unwen.

Huszczo, G. E. (1996). Tools for team excellence. Palo Alto California: Davies-Black Publishing.

Jimenez, D. & Sanz-Valle, R. (2011). Innovation, organizational learning, and performance. Journal of Business Research, 64, 408-417.

Johnson, & Belcher, (1998). Examining the relationship between listening effectiveness and leadership emergence. Small Group Research, 29(4), 452-471.

Jones, G. R., & George, J. M. (1998). The experience and evolution of trust. Academy of Management Review, 23(3), 531-546.

Kahn, W. A. (1990). Psychological conditions of personal engagement and disengagement at work. Academy of Management Journal, 33(4), 692-724.

Lloyd, R. (2008). Discretionary effort and the human domain. The Australian and New Zealand Journal of Organizational Psychology, 1, 22-34.

Maier, N. R. F. & Solem, A. (1952). The contribution of a discussion leader to the quality of group thinking: The effective use of minority opinions. Human Relations, 5, 277-288.

Maslow, A. H. (1954). Motivation and personality. New York: Harper & Row.

Mehrabian. A. (1972). Non-Verbal communication. New Brunswick: AldineTransaction.

Morrison, E. W. & Milliken, F. J. (2000). Organizational silence: A barrier to change and development in a pluralistic world. Academy of Management Review, 25, 706-725.

Morrison, E. W. & Rothman, N. B. (2009). Silence and the dynamics of power. In J. Greenberg, & M. S. Edwards (Eds.), Voice and silence in organizations (pp. 111-133). UK: Emerald Group.

Nichols, R. G. & Lewis, T. R. (1963). Listening and speaking. Dubuque, Iowa: Brown Company.

Slap, S. (2010). Bury my heart in conference room B. New York: Penquin Books.

Tepper, B. J. & Lockhart, D. (2007). Abused subordinates' upward communication" A coping perspective. Journal of Management, 33(3), 261-289.

Tyler, T. R. (1989). The psychology of procedural justice: A test of the group-value model. Journal of Personality and Social Psychology, 57(5), 830-838.

ACKNOWLEDGMENTS

Rob and Christine would like to acknowledge the wisdom, advise and help from so many. First, we owe a debt of gratitude to those hundreds of High-Influence Leaders who influenced us in numerous ways by their writings, teachings, examples and opportunities to work with them.

With respect and appreciation to our *Breaking Corporate Silence* Team, we owe a debt of gratitude to:

· All the research participants who shared the silence experiences openly and honestly.

· Our developmental editor Regina Maruca whose suggestions, feedback and patience over several months were invaluable.

· Margaret Yorganjian and Jessica Rogers Dill who provided a "reader's perspective."

· Kojenwa Moit for her public relations expertise and unwavering energy.

· Cynthia Bourque for graphic design expertise.

· Josh Fertado for his social media focus and advice.

· Jonathan, Cindy and Danielle at Silverstreet for their ideas, hours of consulting and professionalism.

· Our partners and best friends who supported us over an eighteen month time frame: they cooked, took care of us while we wrote this book.

· Our endorsers, each of whom models High-Influence Leadership®.

· David Toth, at Imperial Image for his determination and detail orientation.

· MediaBoss for their energy and devotion to this cause.

· Ben Olson who expeditiously proofread the entire book within a stressful time constraint.

· Our friend and colleague Stan Slap, who was an inspiration throughout this process.

· The Boston College Club for the beautiful launch event venue.

For additional information on *Breaking Corporate Silence*

www.BreakingCorporateSilence.com
Info@breakingcorporatesilence.com

ABOUT THE AUTHORS

DR. ROB BOGOSIAN is the founder and principal consultant at RVB Associates (Boston, Massachusetts and Naples, Florida). The firm provides research-based executive leadership development and consulting services focused on linking management and leadership development to business strategy to achieve and sustain competitive advantage. Prior to establishing RVB Associates, Rob was Vice President of Performance Development at Wachovia, now Wells Fargo Corporation, a global financial services company. Rob served as Professor of Management at Hult International Business School, (formerly Arthur D. Little School of Management) Cambridge, Massachusetts. He is currently an Executive Education Adjunct Faculty Member, Florida Atlantic University, Boca Raton, Florida. Rob holds a BSBA degree in Finance from Suffolk University, Boston, MA, M.Ed. from Boston University and Certificate of Graduate Studies in Organizational Development from Leslie University, Graduate School of Management, Cambridge, MA.

Rob earned his Doctorate in Human and Organizational Development from The George Washington University, Washington, D.C.

www.RVBassociates.com

CHRISTINE MOCKLER CASPER is President of Communication, Motivation & Management, Inc. a consulting firm in Boston, Massachusetts and Cape Haze, Florida. She has spent the past twenty-five years assisting organizations to move forward to breakthrough results. She is a sought after international facilitator, coach, consultant and keynote who enthusiastically conveys information while simultaneously modeling leadership principles necessary for success in today's dynamic economy. Christine has a passion for providing insights and tools to assist in professional and organizational transformation based upon strategies, techniques and thoroughly researched models for excellence. She is frequently interviewed by the media and has been featured on numerous network shows including NBC10, Fox News, NBC Daytime, Good Day New York and NPR. She has held a series of leadership positions within a Fortune 500 company and received her MBA from Northeastern University. Christine is the author of *From Now on with Passion – A Guide to Emotional Intelligence*, and *365 Affirmations for Mastering Stress*.

www.CM-MInc.com